**SING U
A SONG
BEFORE
SAY GOODBYE**

*Heartwarming tales of a young lad growing
up in Liverpool during WW2*

SING US A SONG MA, BEFORE WE SAY GOODBYE

Heartwarming tales of a young lad growing up in Liverpool during WW2

JOHNNY SLATER

and

CAROL WAINWRIGHT

BROWN
DOG
BOOKS

Published under licence by Brown Dog Books and
The Self-Publishing Partnership, 7 Green Park Station, Bath BA1 1JB

www.selfpublishingpartnership.co.uk

ISBN printed book: 978-1-78545-287-1
ISBN e-book: 978-1-78545-288-8

Cover design by Kevin Rylands
Internal design by Tim Jollands

Printed and bound in the UK

CONTENTS

PROLOGUE

When asked about Liverpool most people can easily name our famous football teams, Everton and Liverpool. Many know of Liverpool's fascinating maritime history. And who doesn't know that Liverpool is the birthplace of the legendary Beatles? Four talented musicians who changed the face of music forever, and who immortalised "The Cavern," a small club tucked away in lively Matthew Street in the town's busy centre.

No-one could fail to recognize the warm and humorous voice of a Scouser. Love, strength, and a kind heart are the key qualities of Scousers. Singers, comedians, footballers, actors and actresses, Liverpool births them all.

Not all Scousers are world famous but rest assured, every Scouser is born with a rare and inspiring gift. We can talk the hind leg off a donkey – but when something needs doing we get up and get it done. When a neighbour needs help, we pick up a brush and scrub out, without question. No need for thanks or recognition. We help each other out. We serve because we want to. This remarkable trait is natural. It's in our blood. We make the most of our lot with a song in our heart and a smile on our face. This claim is made proudly, unashamedly, and without arrogance because it's true. A Scouser will find beauty in anything, even when it's not pretty, in good times and bad. We look after each other and count our blessings. We may not have much but what we do have we share and we are thankful. It's as simple as that. Little things mean a lot and we are grateful for whatever cards life has dealt us.

Liverpool today may well be just another port that others pass through on their way to sunnier and exotic destinations. Travellers perhaps only glimpse the northern banks of the River Mersey. How many people notice the shipping and commerce in this thriving and busy port, or witness the countless containers carrying cargo all over the world? The rolling waves of the Mersey are still relied on even if its once thriving Victorian heydays have long since passed. Liverpool was the busiest port in the country during both world wars and its status as a port city has attracted a diverse population, drawn historically from a wide range of peoples, cultures and religions, more particularly, from Ireland and Wales.

Overlooking the River Mersey and dominating one of the world's most famous waterfront skylines is the Royal Liver Building at the Pier Head. Silently perched atop its roof are "Bella and Bertie", the Liver Birds, each carrying a branch of laver seaweed. These iconic birds are made from copper and stand eighteen feet tall with a wingspan of twenty-four feet. Various mythologies surround these legendary creatures, who stand facing away from each other. One such legend has it that the female bird looks out to sea making sure those who sail the waters arrive home safely while the male bird looks towards the city to protect its citizens. Should the birds ever turn to face each other, Liverpool will no longer exist.

On the opposite side of the river is Liverpool's sister port, Birkenhead, and beyond that are the small seaside towns of the Wirral peninsular. Further still is the North Wales countryside, home to many evacuees during World War Two.

Kirkdale is an area of flat land on the banks of the River Mersey, formerly consisting of sand hills, for which this part of the Sefton coast is still well known. It is one of the oldest coastal settlements, pre-dating Liverpool itself. Kirkdale Road was once an important route into Liverpool when the emerging town became a market destination for traders and producers across Lancashire. In 1699 Liverpool became a parish in its own right separating from nearby Walton on the Hill – a separation enforced, according to the history books, by the inability of parishioners to resist the distraction of the Kirkdale Alehouse on their way to church…

Kirkdale was still mostly rural at the beginning of the nineteenth century and was only half-developed by around 1850. But new roads were being added on to Liverpool's northern fringes to cater for the growth in businesses spreading out from Dale Street and Castle Street.

As Liverpool's wealth increased, the richest merchants looked for room to build the large houses that would reflect their status in society. Kirkdale was one of the first areas to become a suburb, and a fashionable one at that. The coast to the west of Kirkdale was, before the arrival of the docks, popular as a destination for bathers and those seeking fresh air. Later, when the Wellington, Huskisson, and Sandon Docks were built, Southport replaced Kirkdale as the preferred holiday destination for discerning Liverpudlians.

A village so close to the ambitious and growing town of Liverpool could not expect to stay rural for very long. As the Industrial Revolution approached, the area of Kirkdale became increasingly more built-up, while two significant nineteenth-century developments put paid to its days as a semi-rural suburb. The first was the Leeds-Liverpool Canal, which brought trade and goods into North Liverpool and immediately attracted a huge number of businesses to its terminus around Leeds Street. The second was the Liverpool & Bury (later the Lancashire & Yorkshire) Railway which opened in 1848. This not only encouraged even more industry into the area, but also helped to transform the mellow atmosphere from one of cut grass and cow dung to a smoky, sooty climate.

Kirkdale's proximity to the docks made it a great place to build houses for the thousands of casual workers who were too poor to live more than walking distance from their potential employers. As Liverpool's growth reached its peak in the late Victorian period, a grid-iron pattern of terraces crept along the landscape. The richer classes –from the clerks all the way up to the shipping line owners moved further away from the town centre. The clerks tended to move to Anfield and Walton while the richest built new villas in the countryside around Woolton and West Derby, or north of Bootle. Kirkdale was one of the earliest suburbs to be incorporated into Liverpool itself, in 1835. The swathes of unsuitable housing which blighted places like Kirkdale in the twentieth century were the inevitable result of unscrupulous landlords throwing up as many properties as possible for the lowest cost.

* * * *

In the middle of this grid-iron pattern stood a group of terraced streets running off the busy Stanley Road and it was in one of these houses on the corner of Stanley Road and Lambeth Road that Emily Slater, thirty-one years old, gave birth to her second son, on 22 January 1933. Emily's husband Jimmy was a Donkeyman in the Merchant Navy, looking after the ships' steam engines since joining up at age fourteen. He was home on leave when the midwife delivered the Slaters' new baby. Emily's eldest son Jimmy, three years old, hearing for the first time the wail of a newborn, wriggled on his Da's knee.

In the tiny kitchen Emily's younger sister, Julia, was hovering, hand on hip and clutching a worn-out tea-towel. Hearing the baby's first cry she sprang into action. Tucking a few loose strands of fiery red hair into a blue flowered turban, she fixed her piercing green eyes on the waiting kettle and the plate of meat-paste butties. Her beloved Emily would be starving, gagging for a strong cup of tea after such a long labour. The two sisters were joined at the hip, quick-witted, running their homes like well-oiled machines. Since leaving school they had worked together at the jam factory, Hartley's, a three-mile tram ride away in Fazakerley. When the babies came along they took separate shifts and shared the care of their children. The threat of more job losses in the factory was looming but they would deal with that when the time came. Strong and resourceful, they would find a way to put food on the table and feed the family.

Julia's husband Matty was in the parlour with Jimmy and the children. Matty scooped up his own three kids, announcing proudly that they had a new cousin to play with.

Matty was a dock labourer and, that day, had joined the hundreds of other men on the dockside since early morning in the hope of picking up at least one day's work. He had been unsuccessful, trailing home dejected yet again. The Great Depression had hit Liverpool hard in the 1930s, leaving thousands of residents unemployed. Traditional roles within the family had changed and men like Matty, finding themselves out of work, had to rely on their wives to help make ends meet. Many did not take the loss of their status as bread winner well. Many of them stopped looking for work, paralyzed by bleak chances and by the destruction of their self-respect. Some became so frustrated that they just walked out on their family completely.

Women like Julia and Emily, on the other hand, found their status enhanced by their new roles. Left with little choice, they went against centuries of opposition to married women working outside the home to help support their families. Their status and power in the home increased, and they gained a new voice in domestic decisions. The Great Depression lasted until 1939, ending only with the boost provided by a war economy.

But 22 January 1933 was a day for the Slater family to put their troubles aside, and celebrate the birth of baby Johnny. Johnny's Da and his Uncle Matty took off to the local pub, The Meddy, and had more than a few jars to wet the new baby's head. (Three-year-old Jimmy would join his little brother Johnny to hear another newborn wail a couple of years later when their sister Cath joined the family, making the Slaters of Kirkdale complete).

Meanwhile, ensconced in their little house, Emily held her new baby son tightly to her and kissed the top of his head while Julia poured that longed-for cup of tea.

"Welcome to our world Johnny, I'm yer Ma."

INTRODUCTION
Carol

Dad leant back in his old easy-chair and sighed heavily. Drifting and dreaming over eighty-four years he glanced at his own footprints marked through the sands of time.

"Yesterdays and yester years," Dad said, "alive and as real as today."

He laughed and closed his eyes. "I've just got a strong whiff of 'Aunt Sally's Disinfectant', luv!" He sniffed the imagined air and chuckled. "A smell from the old days, Carol. Bloody hell, me Ma used to stink the house out with that stuff!" Dad sees the old familiar bottle clearly in his mind.

"She told me it's the only cleaner worth its salt." Dad shook his head at the old memory. "Ma huffed and puffed till her knuckles bled," he grimaced. "Clutching that worn out scrubbing brush and bucket of hers." He studied his reflection in the window, seeing so much more than I could.

"Me Ma had to kneel down slowly 'cos her poor knees were always red raw." Dad winced, remembering the pain on his Ma's face.

"But she would insist on keeping the house immaculate. I can hear her shouting now!" Dad laughed and threw back his head, mimicking her voice.

"We mightn't have much of an 'ouse Johnny, but what we do have we can keep spotlessly clean. Cleanliness is next to godliness."

"Like the other Mums in our street," Dad said, his eyes glistening with pride and tears. "Me Ma was a strong-willed woman. When all else fell apart those women stood together during the war and did what needed to be done for the family.

"They stayed united and defiant through the whole bloody war. Sacrificing their very existence so their children would have a near normal childhood despite a raging invasion."

Dad shuffled the faded photographs from his treasured box of souvenirs.

"The women shared what little they had, Carol, because little things meant a lot. And they expected nothing in return from an uncertain world."

I handed Dad a strong cup of tea as he struggled to keep his tears at bay.

"Me Ma said, 'To wake up and know my children were alive, to see my family, friends and neighbours safe. That's more than enough for us, Johnny.'"

Tears mingled with laughter in those darkest of days.

Dad picked up a stack of crumbling number 16 tram tickets, stroking them fondly. "There's an old song that plays over and over in my heart, Carol. The words are locked in a distant part of my soul." Dad sang an old line from his remembered song with a wistful smile. "It's funny how time slips away." His red eyes well up.

"Time *does* slip away, luv, but some days you can never forget. Like the day we went to war."

Dad drinks his steaming cup of tea. Builders' tea, the colour of creosote, exactly as he likes it.

"Bombings, air raids, ration books, black-out curtains. And who could forget the bloody awful stink of derbac and carbolic soap!" He laughed again and carefully placed the china cup in its saucer.

"That longed-for wail of the all clear siren was like music to our ears in those gloomy air raid shelters."

I can't even begin to imagine the horrors a world at war brings.

"Well, the adults bore the worries, Carol." Dad blew out a long, slow breath. "As odd as it seems luv, life for us kids carried on as a bitter-sweet adventure. Us kids still played ollies," Dad smiled. "We kicked a football, went to the movies, and swapped our comics. We still told ghost stories around a bonfire on the rubble that used to be houses."

Dad kissed the yellow photograph of his brother and sister, Jimmy and Cath, and burst into loud sobs, tears pouring down his face.

"God, I'll never forget that awful feeling in the pit of my belly. Or the wretched voice of the duty Sergeant when he said, 'I'm so sorry, Johnny'. That awful, endless journey home across the North Sea. I cried until there was nothing left inside. My heartache wrung me out until my insides were dry and raw. I wanted to run away, find a dark room and close the curtains, hide away so I wouldn't have to witness life carrying on as usual. How could it when my world had crumbled? The sun still rose and the moon still set. The birds still sang in the trees, but not for me. For me there was no beauty or sweet sound left in the world." Dad clutched the photograph to his heart and shook his head.

"You've got a wonderful memory, Dad," I said, handing him a tissue and picked up his empty cup and saucer. "I know there are some terrible, painful ones but why don't we write a book of *all* your memories, hey, Dad?"

He turned, looked at me and smiled. "Do you think we could *really* write a book, luv? Is it even possible?"

"*Anything's* possible Dad, if you want it enough," I said, jumping up. "Especially when it comes from the heart. Reliving moments of your childhood could help other people taste their own sweet memories. And it will help those who didn't live through the war years understand how community spirit kept people going. Your tales could bring to life the tales other parents and grandparents have told their children."

"Well, luv, those first thirty years growing up in Kirkdale were the happiest of my life," Dad smiled wistfully. "But life hands us choices, different paths we may or may not take. I chose my path, rightly or wrongly. I slung my old guitar over my shoulder, hit the road and moved on.

"But I never forgot the love I shared with my first sweetheart from Kirkdale. My Sweetheart from Snowdrop Street. Love slipped through our fingers somewhere along the way." Dad gazed through the window, sunshine glinting on his silver hair.

"I asked myself many times over the years, Carol, '*Who's kissing her now?*'" Dad sings another old song, the one that means so much to him.

"I wonder if me and my first sweetheart will ever have the chance to leave older footprints across the sands of time. What do you think, luv?"

CHAPTER 1

SOMETHING IN THE AIR

3 September 1939

It wasn't far off my seventh birthday, but I really wanted to be eight! I just really, really, wanted to be *older*! Lenny next door was eight and at least three inches taller. He bragged about being the oldest. We'd been off school for a few days with a cold but today was Sunday, so it felt like we'd had a long holiday. Ma said we'd caught the same bug and could do with a few more days' rest. Ma was minding Lenny while his Mum was catching up on some sleep. She worked two jobs, mornings in the jam factory with me Ma and Aunty Julia and afternoons in the tobacco factory on Commercial Road. The B.A.T. stunk to high heaven and the smell clung to Lenny's mum's white overalls but she didn't seem to notice. Ma said it didn't matter, people were lucky to get their hands on any kind of work never mind what yer smelt like! Ma noticed the thin spitting rain had blown over and once again the sun shone brightly. She was itching to chuck us outside.

"A bit of fresh air will do yer the world of good. It'll put a bit of colour in yer cheeks and give you an appetite. *An' take the dogs with yer!*" she yelled from the white-tiled sink in our little back kitchen. I didn't need fresh air to give me an appetite. The dogs went berserk, manic with the possibility of a new adventure.

Me Ma and Aunty Julia had rescued our stray dogs Punch and Judy a while back now. Saved them from starvation.

"To tell you the truth, Emily, your Punch has got a face only a mother could love," spluttered Aunty Julia, choking on a cup of treacle-like tea. We'd run out of milk again.

"Well!" puffed Ma, lifting an eyebrow, "I think I'd be right in sayin' that your Judy's got a bum on her like a bag of washin'." She tittered, but a look of indignation remained fixed on her face.

"*Pffft,*" Aunty Julia took a long drag on her ciggy. "I'm gonna tell yer somethin' for nothin', our Emily. These bloody daft dogs landed on their paws the day they found me and you. A pair of soft ollies, that's what they think you an' me are, luv. Look at the fat bellies on them! Spoilt bloody rotten. Yer wouldn't think they were the same dogs, would yer, queen?"

Ma nodded and smiled down at Punch. Her face was blushed rosy, unwrinkled as any young girl's even though she would soon be forty. Years of struggle and hardship, bringing up myself, my big brother Jimmy and my little sister Cath had perhaps added some fine lines to the corners of her sparkly green eyes, but you could hardly notice unless you were close up. Her skirts and dresses were second-hand and usually the wrong size, held up by huge safety pins. She always kept herself smart, clean and tidy, often saying to me "Do I look alright, Johnny? Don't want anyone thinkin' I've just stepped out of Ann Fowler's,[1] eh, luv?"

But Ma always looked beautiful to me, even though she'd not bought herself anything new since before she married my Da. While he was away at sea Ma made ends meet bottling jams every day and taking in washing with Aunty Julia once a week.

"Poor little buggers," tutted Aunty Julia, rubbing her feet over the dogs' bellies. She slurped the last dregs of cold, dark tea and carefully placed the chipped cup upside down on a cracked saucer which didn't quite match.

"They had no more meat on them than a bag of old bones!" Aunty Julia shook her head and stuck a thin hand on her hip. She pulled herself up slowly and rested the pink flowered cup and green saucer on top of the china cabinet. She smoothed the white lace doily

---

[1] 'Ann Fowler's' was a refuge for women on Netherfield Road, about a quarter of a mile from our house. It was demolished in the 1980s, the new refuge now standing on the site of the old Shakespeare Theatre on Frazer Street.

underneath, checking it wasn't curled up. "I'll read our tea leaves in a bit, eh, Emily?"

"Yis please, luv. An' make it bleedin' well more cheerful than the last reading, Julia!"

Aunty Julia blew out a stream of smoke and snubbed out her skinny rollie in a cracked, ash-filled saucer. Ma leaned over to give Punch one more chest rub and kissed the top of his head. I spotted Ma *and* Aunty Julia sneaking Punch *another* stale biscuit.

Ma and Aunty Julia were acting a bit funny today. The pair of them kept glancing at the clock above the fireplace and fiddling about with the wireless, making sure it was tuned-in properly. And they kept giving each other sideway glances. Normally they would be cracking jokes and telling funny tales. They were good at that. And singing and dancing while Ma played the piano. Everyone loved me Ma and Aunty Julia. *Always good for a laugh*, our neighbours said, *the life and soul of any party*. But they weren't laughing today. Something was definitely wrong with the pair of them.

"Out yer go, lads, an' 'urry up or it'll be teatime before yer've had a good play. Get yer legs shifted. Me an yer Aunty Julia have got somethin' important to listen to on the wireless an I don't want yer big ears listenin' in an interruptin'…" Ma stood up and ushered me and Lenny up off the floor.

"Come 'ead, Punch!" I tutted, with a cob on. "…You too, Judy!" We scarpered down our hall to the open front door. And out we flew, ready for a boss game of 'kick the can' with a rusty can of beans rolling in the gutter.

Lenny booted the old can down our gloomy back entry. The dogs went hell for leather, paws not touching the ground. Next door's marmalade tom cat scarped up Mr Moore's old pigeon loft, spitting and hissing. The early morning drizzle had darkened the crumbling backyard walls and now the bricks looked shiny, like someone had coated them in a thick lick of varnish.

Footsteps shuffled behind me and I felt hot, malty breaths trickle down my neck. I turned to see big yellow teeth grinning like a Cheshire Cat.

"Eh, Johnny lad, haven't yer got any school today?"

"Don't be daft, Monk!" I laughed. "It's Sunday, school's closed!" Me and Lenny tittered as Monk Murphy swayed back and forth on huge, fat feet. No doubt he was on his way up to the Lighthouse for an early start on the Guinness. His gangly arms lunged for my shoulder. You could set your clock by old Monk Murphy. He staggered up and down to the Lighthouse *every* day at *exactly* the same time. "An early Guinness keeps the grey hairs on me chest all nice and warm-like." Monk Murphy sang to his own tune. He was a nice, kind man, all six foot four of him. By no means soft, he put the wind up many a hard man, especially on a Saturday night outside the pubs on Stanley Road. A tell-tale ring of yellowed froth, probably from a bottle of stout he'd already chugged for his breakfast, looked sticky on his chapped top lip. He swore it gave his blood the iron that made him strong.

Something strange suddenly struck me. A peculiar feeling in the air. Time suddenly slipped away like milk running from a broken bottle. And then it stood still, frozen. Monk Murphy looked up, tilted his head and took a step back. In a muffled voice he murmured, "Oh, Jesus, Mary and Joseph. Please God, not again!"

Stifled cries and muted thuds reached my ears and a high-pitched wail screamed through the streets. I glanced up quickly at the darkened sky. I could no longer hear what Monk was saying but I saw his mouth move into a scream. It joined those of the others who had appeared out of nowhere.

"JOHNNY, JOHNNY! GET IN THE HOUSE, NOW!"

I heard Ma's frantic cry, but I couldn't see her anywhere. It felt like the sky had clouded over. What looked like a hundred mothers exploded into the street, all of them screaming for the kids to get inside. Ma's voice finally reached me, and I spotted her face. Panic gripped me and I couldn't breathe. I couldn't move. *What was going on? What was happening?*

The siren's wail was deafening. I turned to glimpse Monk's face. He was biting the inside of his lip, skin now grey and pale. A cold sweat dripped into my eyes, stinging and blurring my vision. All I could take in was a mass of mums like a swarm of mosquitos, too quick to see, too noisy to hear. And I could smell the growing fear, sour and rotten. For a second I stood frozen. I tried to swallow the lump stuck in my throat. I had no idea which way to turn. And then I heard me Ma.

"JOHNNY! JOHNNY! WHERE'S OUR JIMMY? GET INSIDE SON, THE BLOODY WORLD'S GONE TO WAR. GET IN, NOW"

I spun around just as my brother came hurtling around the corner. He grabbed me and Lenny and dragged us into our house. Punch and Judy charged behind, whining, scared stiff. Limp tails hung between little legs, scampering towards the safety of home. That siren wailed unmercifully long on that awful day. The day the world went to war.

* * * *

It is probably true to say that almost everyone in Britain was listening to the wireless on the morning of Sunday, 3 September 1939. The wireless had become the oracle through which the nation was to learn its fate. The voice of the BBC in 1939 was Alvar Lidell, a measured, cultivated tone, calm and authoritative. Lidell announced, "In about two minutes, the Prime Minister will broadcast to the nation. Please stand by."

People braced themselves for the worst, most sat huddled in ordinary front rooms across the country. In those two long minutes it was time for older listeners to remember the blight and deaths and deep wounds of the First World War, time for the prescient to call up regrets for the British non-interference in Spain, a lost opportunity, perhaps, to check the fascists; time for a few to curse the policy of Appeasement, and for many to be forced to ponder on the headlines of the previous two days, which had reported the heavy civilian bombing of Poland by the Germans.

Already, the entire population of Britain had gas masks in case Hitler launched a poisonous gas attack. Mass evacuation plans for children were under way. Back garden bomb shelters were being built. In the blue skies on that idyllic late-summer Sunday morning, as the churches emptied their larger-than-usual numbers for the early services, barrage balloons floated high, as if announcing a party.

At 11.15 the Prime Minister, Neville Chamberlain, delivered his speech from the Cabinet Room of 10 Downing Street, struggling to keep the anguish from his voice.

"This morning, the British Ambassador in Berlin handed the German government a final note, stating that unless we heard from them, by 11 o'clock, that they were prepared at once to withdraw their troops from Poland, a state of war would exist between us."

Then came the words most feared by all.

"I have to tell you now that no such undertaking has been received and that, consequently, this country is at war with Germany."

The greatest and most destructive war in history had begun. Fifty-five million lives would be lost, and waiting for us in the near future lay the Holocaust, the atom bomb, the making and breaking of empires and nations. The world would change utterly – all foretold in that grave announcement on a Sunday morning 79 years ago.

CHAPTER 2

FED UP

TO THE BACK TEETH

1 October 1940

Aunty Julia looked up at the dull grey clouds and frowned. After days of blue skies, the threat of a piddle down was lurking among the crumbling chimneys of the terraced houses.

The ravages of war and the inevitable changes to ordinary life were slowly taking their toll. The mothers in our terraced street in Liverpool were drained and weary, living on their nerves. The country had been at war for a year now and the certainty of worse to come lay heavy in everyone's heart. The women constantly worried and feared for their children. Money was tight, food scarce, jobs hard to come by. As the country struggled to adapt to changes, nerves and tempers had become frayed and tattered. Nobody had much but they did have each other, and the women clung on tightly to that one constant. Men and women were witnessing things no-one should ever have to see. Those left at home were doing whatever it took to keep the home fires burning, pulling together to feed the children, putting food on the table against all odds. Getting up after nights of sorrow, heavy, weary and bruised to the bone. Morale was low.

"Goin' to bloody Hell in a handcart, we are," said Aunty Julia. She thrust both hands on each slender hip of her blue aproned frame. A bottle of sticky syrup of figs poked over the top of her apron's overly large pocket. Julia was held up by slim, stocking-less legs as she shuffled bunioned feet irritably in a pair of her husband Matty's tatty grey slippers.

Mothers proud to be 'donkey-stoning' the steps
till they shone nice and bright.

Me Ma glanced up from the white door step she was sweating over with a donkey stone.

"Who is?" Ma eased herself upright on to the cracked pavement.

"England! *And* his bleedin' dog!"

Ma adjusted her green turban and two pink rollers came loose, dangling by a few strands of bright red hair in the middle of her face. She brushed them aside and lit up a hand rolled ciggy so thin you'd think it was a matchstick.

"I know what yer mean, luv," Ma puffed out a curly stream of bluish smoke and sighed heavily. "And the worst is yet to come," she whispered. "I can feel it in me bones…"

Ma and Aunty Julia's words hung in the air for a moment.

'Three Little Fishes' blared out from Mr and Mrs McGrady's ancient gramophone further down the street. Their door was wide open. They were scrapping like cats again. It was unusual at this time of the morning. Normally it was a Friday or Saturday night that witnessed the backlash from a couple of vicious, drunken tongues. Mind you, you wouldn't dream anything had gone on when they woke up next morning. All smiles, and sweetness and light.

Our neighbours twitched their tatty black-out curtains one by one, their prying eyes anxious to figure out what Julia's latest commotion on the doorstep was all about.

Mrs Ellis was the first to appear, striding towards the house purposefully, to get the low-down on Julia's rant. She was a small, wispy woman in her late twenties, and quiet as a mouse unless she had a few gins – then everyone was her best friend and she loved the whole street.

Mrs Moore and Mrs Murphy linked arms, warm winter coats trailing a strong smell of mothballs behind them. They scuttled up the street in perfect time, marching to the beat of their own drum. Deep lines furrowed their foreheads above pursed, pale lips. Each clutched a can of sweetened, condensed milk.

The one-legged pigeon *still* sat on the gutter of the house opposite Ma's, keeping a beady green eye on the goings on in our street. Next door's marmalade moggy gnashed his sharp teeth and sat as still as a statue on the kerb, both eyes glued to the pigeon. His tail twitched in slow motion.

Mr Tom Bradley, a short wiry man with a shaved head, slowly drifted up the street. Humming one of his own songs, twiddling his thumbs over and over. Constantly looking back over his shoulder. We had to cut him some slack, everyone said. He fought in the Great War and witnessed things beyond anyone's imagination. He was a tormented soul and often had nightmares, screaming in the small hours of the morning, escaping into the street, dripping in sweat, shaking, running wild from God knew what.

"He served his country and it destroyed him," Ma said sadly. "No-one will ever know what's really going on in his mind, Johnny. Such a waste. Such a bloody shame." Ma sighed and drooped her eyes. I didn't really understand but I did know it really upset me Ma. She said a prayer for him every single night.

The slam of number 77's door brought Mrs Mitchell flying

towards Ma and Aunty Julia. Head down, her fast little legs went like the clappers, skirting the ugly black-and-white mutt in her path with practiced ease.

They were all there now. The neighbours. Ma said "if yer sneezed in yer backyard toilet yer could be sure one of the neighbours would appear with a hanky". They gathered around me Ma and Aunty Julia.

Mrs Berry's voice crackled out of thin lips. "What's rattled yer cage, Julia?"

"I can't bloody well take it any more!" Julia crushed out her ciggy as if it was a filthy, black cockroach. She sighed and turned sad eyes to the crowd.

The neighbours glanced at each other, worried sick.

"We all need a bloody good cheerin' up." Ma stifled a sob.

"I mean, just look at the state of our bloody faces! Like a dollop of mortal sins, the lot of us." Ma looked weary.

"I tell yer what," snarled Aunty Julia with a flush of renewed spirit "Hitler can bloody well sod off!" Her statement was bold yet it didn't make much more noise than a snapped twig.

The country might have been in the grips of fear, but it was time Elstow Street packed up their troubles and had a good old knees-up.

"Time for us to roll out a barrel, eh? It's been too bloody long," Ma had the hint of a smile creeping in. The glint in Aunty Julia's rebellious green eyes made a come-back.

"*I've got it!*" screamed Aunty Julia, stumbling on the kerb. "A bommy for the kids and jars out for us!"

"Have yer gone bleedin' crackers, Julia? What about the ban? The bloody A.R.P.[2]* will marmalize us, never mind the friggin' Luftwaffe!" Mrs Boyle's beady eyes nearly popped out of her head.

---

[2] Guy Fawkes Night and fireworks were banned immediately at the outbreak of war. Gunpowder was needed for the war effort and bonfires contravened the blackout. The tradition of Guy Fawkes Night had been put on hold throughout the country for however long the war lasted. * Air Raid Patrol.

"Oh, sod the bloody lot of them!" snapped Ma. "All these rules are gettin' on me bloody nerves. They can all just piss off."

Ma stretched out her arms and glared at our neighbours. They stood in silence, thinking, wondering... *How?* It was the question hovering on everyone's lips.

"Surely we can sort somethin' out between the lot of us?" Ma pleaded. "It's not like we've only got half a brain each. Come on, get yer bloody thinkin' 'eads on!"

The rag man from Beatrice Street in nearby Bootle rumbled up the street with his handcart. Puffing out 'Little Brown Jug' on his trumpet he startled the one-legged pigeon. It took off over the roof and next door's moggy bolted, letting out a fart that smelt worse than boiled cabbage gone bad.

"I've got it!" Aunty Julia danced around next door's battered pram. "Let's have a bommy with a difference!" she howled. "An afternoon bommy!"

"They can't shoot us for that, can they?" asked Ma. "They'll never find out."

"It'll have to be a *small* bommy in the street. An' we better make sure the fires *well* out before dusk. Can't risk g'ttin' another fine from the bleedin' A.R.P. Better not show even a glint of light," Aunty Julia was three steps ahead.

"No-one but us lot will even know about it if we just keep our bloody mouths shut," Mrs Moore winked.

"A little fire in a dustbin?" pondered Ma.

"An' anyway, it's still light till about half-past six. The bloody Germans 'aven't got a cat in hells chance of clockin' our bommy. We'll have *loads* of time to 'ave a few laughs an' let our hair down. The kids will love it," said Mrs Ellis, a gummy smile on her face.

"An' what with schools only bein' open in the bleedin' mornin's, the timin's spot on." The neighbours' excitement grew, along with Aunty Julia's and me Ma's.

"We can throw in a few spuds and chestnuts before we burn the auld-arse Guy," laughed Mrs Murphy, rubbing her bony hands on an antwacky[3] dress.

"The kids are gonna be *made up* makin' an auld-arse, *secret* Guy! Even if they can't have bleedin' fireworks," Mrs Moore's cheeks flushed pink.

Mrs Boyle fumbled with an old sweet in her apron pocket. Pulling fluff off a chocolate lime she mumbled, "We'll have to keep our gobs shut." She popped in the sticky sweet sucking loudly and slobbered down her chin. Mrs Boyle hadn't had an easy life. She'd spent most of it in a workhouse in south Liverpool. Her whole family had been torn apart and separated. She had no idea of the whereabouts of her parents, brother or sister. Sorrow found her once again not long after she moved to Kirkdale. Her two children and husband were killed in a house fire while visiting her mother in-law. She could easily have fallen apart, but she fought back. Every day, she fought back hard and chose to see the good things in life, and to make people laugh.

"Not a word to *anyone* outside this bloody street," warned Aunty Julia, eyebrows touching her nose and her long finger wagging. "No blaggin' yer 'eads off down the shops. Are yer listenin' to me? Otherwise, we'll all be seein' our arse." Everyone went silent and nodded.

* * * *

Conducted on doorsteps and issued with top secret warnings, meetings of minds and mop-heads became the new order of the day. It was planned to the nth degree. The street would have their daytime bommy on Halloween, making it a joint celebration with duck apple night.

"God love us, but isn't it about time we took a few risks and had a laugh? Who the hell knows what's waitin' around the corner?" said

---

[3] Antwacky = old-fashioned.

me Ma, straightening out her faded pinny.

"Yer right, Emily," agreed Mrs Boyle. "We could be a long time looking at a bloody lid."

Mrs Boyle teetered with one foot on the edge of the kerb. She spat her words out that quick her top set of yellowed teeth flew out, smack bang into the path of Punch who was chasing next door's moggy. Mrs Boyle made a grab for the teeth before Punch ate them. The marmalade moggy took advantage of the distraction and escaped through the window of Mrs Kelly's front room. Her aspidistra crashed off the table. The moggy spat and hissed. Soil and leaves scattered all over Mrs Kelly's square piece of second-hand brown carpet, as rough as the bottom of a budgie's cage. Punch howled in misery as he failed to catch that bloody cat, *again*. The cat laughed, as only cats can.

Mrs Kelly was bloody fuming; Mrs Boyle went arse over tit. "It's a bloody good job me bum's that big I haven't done meself a long-term injury. Bleedin' cats and dogs!" she spluttered, trying her best to stuff the teeth back in her head. No harm done except perhaps the loss of Mrs Boyle's dignity, and to be fair, Mrs Kelly's aspidistra was never *quite* the same again.

* * * *

"Shared joy is a double joy,
Shared sorrow is half a sorrow."

We kids were made up having a street secret. Like spies and secret agents, we got stuck in and made our own plans, sworn to secrecy so the A.R.P. wouldn't get wind of our bommy. Warnings came with the threat of a clout around the ear and Da's slipper across the backside.

We wheeled around a sorry-looking Guy for a couple of weeks, sitting cock-eyed in an ancient wicker bath chair with its arse hanging out. The bath chair probably once belonged to Paddy Kelly from Flinders Street whose feet were that big if you threw his shoe in the Mersey it would be a shipping hazard. Paddy Kelly collected all manner of strange things.

We'd done alright, us kids, getting the odd penny here and there. At least we had enough between us for a handful of treats – a packet of sherbet and a few sticks of liquorice. A dozen pin-wheels and rip-raps would have been better but, seeing as fireworks were banned, we had no chance of stumbling across any. Even Lenny couldn't find any and he could normally find all kinds of things. Most fell of the back of a lorry, me Ma said, usually on Stanley Road. I reckoned it must have been very bumpy along Stanley Road.

We spent hours and hours knocking up our 'Guy'. A holey old brown jumper from next door's Dad, a pair of Oxford trousers from the old fella at number twenty-four. The fly didn't have any buttons and they had patches on patches.

"They're not a blind bit of good to my feller any more. Yer might as well take 'em. I'll be glad to see the back of them, to tell yer the truth, they stink out me wardrobe like a sweaty old alehouse!" The old fella's wife was chuffed to bits.

We grabbed them and scarpered in case the old fella showed up. They could have been his favourite trousers for all we knew. Lenny 'found' two broken brush handles outside the chandlers on Stanley Road.

"Don't think the chandler wanted them anymore," smirked Lenny. Tied together they made a skeleton frame. We stuffed him with rags and newspapers and a pair of old bloomers from Mrs.Moore. She had ears like an elephant and could hear a whisper a mile off. Her washing line was pegged out with at least two pairs of ugly bloomers every bloody day.

"God knows what she does with all them knickers," blagged me Ma and Aunty Julia. They looked like a ship's sail to me, blowing in a storm.

An old burst football made a great head for our auld-arse Guy, topped with a docker's old flat cap found by Lenny down one of the entries on Stanley Road. Ma thought it was probably lost by a drunk on his way home from The Lighthouse. The lanky lady with a posh voice from number seventeen gave us a dirty white silk muffler past its best. Nobody round here had mufflers but she obviously beat a different kettle of fish. Aunty Julia said our auld-arse Guy had the kind of face that'd make a cat laugh. Ma said he looked like a slapped kipper and Mrs Boyle hooted, "he's gorra face like a two-bob piss-pot. Pure white, but chipped as 'ell!" We couldn't wait to chuck him on the dustbin fire.

There'd be songs in the street. Some games: Bulldog, Ip Dip, The Big Ship Sails… and hot potatoes and chestnuts on the fire. Our Cath tapping the feet off herself. She'd been clicking her heels to 'The Chattanooga Choo Choo' all week. She couldn't half dance, our Cath.

And we'd have Duck Apple too: Ma's row of shiny red apples strung from one wall to the other. Apples dangling in mid-air. Ma blindfolded us with torn-up shirt sleeves and tied our hands behind our back with tatty tea towels. We'd try to sink our teeth into unseen apples, which refused to stay still, ducking our heads in an old tin bath of freezing cold water. Apples bobbing like boats in a lake. Apples everywhere, except in the mouth. Punch with his nose and paws in the bath doing some sort of doggy paddle. The wet dog smell that lingered for days.

CHAPTER 3

SCHOOL-YARD SHENANIGANS

31 October, 1940 (Bommy Day)

"JOHNNY!"

I spun around.

"OVER 'ERE, SOFT LAD!"

I clocked his daft head first. Squashed between the rusty gates of Daisy Street School.

A bitter cold wind turned his watery eyes red. Clenched white knuckles rattled the old iron bars.

I legged it over to my older brother. A stink of fried kippers followed me. Or was it the howling wind dragging up a cold, wet, fish smell across the murky, rolling waves of the Mersey?

Uneven bumps of broken black tarmac slowed me down, as did the six hundred skinny elbows shoving and pushing me out of the way.

Barbara and Ellen, skinny sisters who spoke to no-one except each other, swung four black pigtails and skipped towards the gate. I noticed there was only one red ribbon between them. Brown, frayed ropes slapped the ground. Four dirty grey pumps held up baggy, holey socks that were probably once white. They were bowed quite prettily, with string laces.

The unsmiling sisters crashed into me. I ended up flat on my face in a crumpled heap on the gritty, cold ground. Rolling over, I looked up to see the sisters' upside-down skipping ropes still slapping the ground. I heard two muffled tuts and caught a scowl from the older sister, Ellen. Matching blue dresses, like parachutes, blew up in the air and I glimpsed an eyeful of baggy navy knickers. And the sky was as grey and dull as old Mrs Murphy's lace bloomers.

"The big ship sails on the ally-ally-oh…"

The sisters had been singing that bloody song all morning. I scrambled on to all fours and brushed off tiny bits of stone embedded in my knees and hands. I glanced around the playground. Some kids were still lagging behind, but now heading for the gates quickly, desperate for a taste of freedom. Ma said we reminded her of a forgotten pan of scouse bubbling over.

"You'd think you kids didn't have a minute to spare," she tutted. "Looks like a yard brush has swept a pile of old rubbish off a top-heavy table when you lot come spillin' out of school at home time!"

Big Billy, the tough lad from Reading Street, was leaning on the toilet block, where more broken, brown bricks crumbled away each day. Scratching his greasy, long black hair he snarled, red-faced, with clenched green teeth. He glared, face yellow-red and spotty, at three younger, freckled, coatless boys whose eyes remained firmly on the ground, shuffling their feet like nervous sheep, trembling with fear in front of the cock of our school.

Our sour-faced headmistress charged towards Big Billy, her heavy leather boots clicking across the yard like the castanets Spanish ladies danced with, or so me Da said. Her long black coat caught on a gust of wind and flapped wildly behind her like a Devil's billowing cape.

He's in for it now, I smiled to myself. Serves him right! Bloody bullyin' bugger should pick on someone his own size for a change.

"JOHNNY! *JOHNNY!* I SAID, HURRY UP!"

"Jesus, Mary and Joseph!" I turned to clumsy Compass dozily dawdling by. He had earned his nickname from Monk Murphy on account of his nose sniffing North while his eyes stared South. He was a bit of a shrimp, really, and couldn't punch a hole in a wet echo, but Christ knows he had a mouth the size of Birkenhead. All puff and no wind. The first thing you noticed about Compass was the size of his feet.

"Look at the state of our Jimmy's face!" I turned to Compass, hands screwed up tightly in my pocket. "He's got his knickers in a twist again," I muttered under my breath, shaking my head. Compass was oblivious: too busy struggling with his cousin's overcoat, the inside-out sleeve tripped him up as he tried to turn it the right way round.

All in a twist, Compass accidentally dropped his ollies[4] and let out a high-pitched wail, like next door's cat. His prized collection of brightly coloured ollies scattered all over the playground. His best one, the parrot, was heading straight for the grid-hole. I dropped to my knees in a bid to save his red and white parrot before it was swallowed up by the deep sewers of Liverpool. Our Jimmy, though, was glaring at me, arms crossed in front of his chest with a look that would sour a lemon.

"I tell you what, me laddo," he roared through the bars of the school gate (I couldn't help but roll my eyes – Jimmy sounded more like me Da every day), "you'd better get tidied up before we get home, lad! That head of yours looks like an October cabbage." He leaned back a little and continued moaning, like an old fella with a cob on.[5] "If me Ma or Aunty Julia clocks you lookin' like that there'll be murder. Making a holy show of us, yer are."

Jimmy was bossy and not half fussy. Ma said it was because he was older and had his eye on the girls. I didn't know anything about that but anyway, right now, he was giving me daggers.

"We've got werk to do, tatty-head!" he yelled, turning as red as a turkey cock. "That load of old wood in our backyard won't shift itself, yer know! Let's get it in the dustbin for the bommy before me Ma collars us to do something else. And I need to take your Punch for a quick walk down Pluto Street on a message."

Aha! I *knew* it! The real reason Jimmy was in a manic rush was *Amy* – the curly haired girl from Pluto Street. "She's got the face of

[4] Ollies = marbles
[5] cob on = in a temper

an angel," Jimmy was fond of telling us. It was all *Amy this* and *Amy that* in our house these days. I was fed-up to the back teeth with his sloppy, cissy talk.

"AND I've got to get to the library," Jimmy droned on and on. "Me encyclopaedias are due. Hurry *up*, will yer!"

Jimmy was a bookworm and knew everything about anything. Ma said he'd read the back of a ciggy pack if there was nothing else to grab him.

"You'll end up with glasses like the bottom of a Guinness bottle, mark my words Jimmy. Straining your eyes with all that little print." Ma warned him every single day but he didn't take a blind bit of notice. He just rolled his blue eyes and peered at the cracks in the ceiling. Jimmy wanted to know *everything* about the whole bloody world and travel the seven seas.

My hands were all mucky, what with those bloody pig-tailed sisters knocking me flat on me face. I spat into them anyway, ignoring the muck, to flatten me hair. Better make an effort to shut our Jimmy up. Straggly bits of fringe got on my nerves. Poking me in the eye and sticking up like Pansy Potter. I suddenly remembered my Beano sat at home on the easy chair. I was made up whenever I got hold of a new pile of comics to leaf through. Just me and Punch. He'd sit on my knee, cock his head and paw through the pages. Ma said we made a pretty picture, what with that one odd ear of his being bigger than the other an all. He was soft as putty, our Punch. *Daft as a brush*, said our neighbours.

Our Jimmy closed in on me. "For God's sake, Johnny, pull yer kecks up! Yer look like you've got both legs in one knicker!"

I quickly pulled up my second-hand shorts. They were about two sizes too big and always falling down. I didn't have a belt of my own and it was our Jimmy's turn to wear it this week. Ma said I always looked that scruffy at the end of the day – even the rag-man wouldn't take me. But what did I care? I had far too much exploring to do to worry about what I looked like.

I bent down and tied the broken lace on my old scuffed boot. Wiggling sore toes, I straightened out the cardboard curling up beneath my baggy grey sock. The holes in my boots stretched bigger each day and the cardboard was as much use as a chocolate tea-pot.

"You need them re-soled," said Ma. "But yer'll 'ave to hang on. I 'aven't got a carrot to me name this week. When I've got a few bob, I'll take yer up to the cobblers on Lemon Street. Right now, Johnny, if suits were a penny I couldn't afford a sleeve."

I hobbled slowly towards Jimmy and ducked a few inches only *just* missing the smack aimed at my lughole.

"Aww, eh, Jimmy, give yer chin a rest…" I stuck out my tongue, barrelling in front of him but fell over my own two feet.

Jimmy threw back his head and laughed. "Serves you bloody well right," he spluttered.

"Yer hard-faced git!" I rubbed my bleeding knee. It'd be a pig's foot in the morning. "I'm tellin' me Ma on you, Jimmy!"

* * * *

Me and Jimmy raced around the corner of our street, heads down, breathless and desperate for the bommy to get started. Jimmy pulled up suddenly. I stumbled to the side and threw out my hand instinctively to brace my fall in case I crashed into his back. He grabbed my shoulder and put his hand over his mouth and pressed hard, as though trying to hold a scream inside. A battered old hand cart sat gawping miserably outside our house.

"I hope that doesn't mean what I think it means," sighed Jimmy. The sky turned grey and the low moan of a foghorn crept slowly up our street. Jimmy's bony shoulders slumped.

"What d'yer mean, Jimmy?" I went cold. Somewhere in the street a baby cried. A door slammed. Next door's moggy wailed. The one-legged pigeon cooed dolefully.

The foghorn moaned on, relentlessly. Calm and serene on the surface but simmering underneath, like lava bubbling in a dormant volcano. A feeling in my gut told me something was brewing.

Manny Cohen, owner of the pawn shop, slunk silently past. His dog with no tail glanced the other way. Manny shoved his hands deep into the pockets of baggy black trousers too short in the leg. One strap of his red striped braces had snapped. He raised a bushy white eyebrow, peering over round, gold-framed glasses, gave a sly, sideways glance at the handcart, and tutted. Mrs Ellis twitched her blackout curtains.

Our front door flew wide open and Ma bounced over the two steps.

"What's the bloody old handcart for, Ma?" Jimmy turned towards Ma.

"Get in the 'ouse, I'll tell yiz in a minute. Keep an eye on Cath."

"But Ma, what's it *for*?" Jimmy kicked a stone and huffed and puffed.

Ma wasn't listening. She pounded on Mrs Boyle's wooden front door with the heel of her fist.

"*WHAT'S IT FOR, MA?*" Jimmy carried on yelling down the street. I pulled me kecks up.

"I said I'll tell yiz in a minute," Ma shrieked back, glancing over her shoulder. "I told yer I won't be long, I've just got a few favours to ask of the neighbours."

"Come on, Johnny," Jimmy sighed, and we trudged into our house.

God knows what Ma's got up her sleeve, I muttered to Punch, who'd leapt on my knee.

Jimmy threw himself on to the floor next to Cath, muttering and mumbling under his breath. He kissed the top of Cath's head. Her tongue stuck out; pasting bits of wool and buttons on to an old doll with no eyes or hair she was concentrating hard. The flour and water glue were up to her elbows and smeared all over her once pink dress. Jimmy ruffled her red curls and said, "Ma's got something planned for us Cath, but it'll turn out good, just you wait and see." He was wise, our Jimmy, but his face didn't look convinced.

"I wonder what's going on, Jimmy?" I leapt out of the chair to pull back Cath who was just about to grab hold of Ma's second-hand curtains. She'd only just got them and would have a canary fit if they got splattered in glue.

Ma came bursting through the door like there was no tomorrow. I looked across at her, unsure what to say or do. She kept quiet as she slipped into comfy old slippers with holes in the toes.

"We're on the move!" She blurted out, as she dropped heavily into the easy chair. Punch whimpered and slid under the table. I glanced over at Jimmy, bewildered. My mouth had gone dry.

"I bloody well knew it!" shouted Jimmy. "Why, Ma, why?"

Cath let out a grating squeal like someone had trod on a mouse.

I looked over at Ma and clocked more of them bloody plants on the windowsill behind her. Ma kept bringing them home from the butcher on Stanley Road. He grew them in something called an allotment. *Mint*, me Ma said. The leaves stunk like a dead man's fingers. I moved over to our Jimmy, sprawled out on the floor, hands behind his head. Punch followed me and flopped over the two of us.

"*Why* are we moving, Ma?" I whined with Punch.

"Again!" Jimmy snarled.

"I don't want to move, Ma!" I stifled a sob.

"Neither do I," cried Cath.

"Not again Ma, not again," Jimmy rolled over on to his belly and sighed. Punch hid his head under my knee.

Ma could see the disappointment in our faces.

"I don't *want* to move, Ma," I repeated "What about me mates?" My mouth tasted like I'd swallowed cod liver oil and malt.

Jimmy crawled over to the cupboard and pulled out an old dish cloth that was once a bed sheet and wiped Cath's hands. He then picked up a book from the sideboard and let out a big sigh.

I kicked off my boot, and Punch lunged after it. I didn't care if he chewed it to bits. I didn't *want* to move house again. Nanny Slater said Ma was like a gypsy, all itchy feet she couldn't scratch. Whenever my Da came home from sea he had to visit his own Mum first to find out where we were living.

"Oh, cheer up, you lot! Look at the miserable gobs on yer!" laughed Ma. "Yer'll still be able to see all yer mates. We're only movin' around the corner, to Flinders Street! Next door to yer Aunty Julia! It's gonna be great, kids, just you wait and see. *And*," – she was smiling like she'd found a gold clock – "I've borrowed that old handcart for the whole of the weekend! It's big enough to get our new piano in!"

"A piano, Ma?" squealed Cath.

"A PIANO?" me and Jimmy roared.

The three of us leapt up and threw ourselves on top of Ma. Moans and groans about moving house vanished into thin air. Good old Ma! You could bank on me Ma to have a surprise tucked up her sleeve.

"Oh yis," she grinned and shoved her bum up a bit to make room for us on the easy chair. "I bagged us a bargain in Mrs Turnbull's second-hand shop in Brisbane Street. Our piano will be the talk of the wash-house! I'll give yer a song at the bommy,"

We couldn't care less about moving house now. Not now we'd got a piano.

"Plus…" said Ma, "I've got a big gang of helpin' hands to shift our stuff in the mornin'."

Me and Jimmy blew out a sigh of relief.

Home Sweet Home.

"You two lads will still have to weigh in a bit and give us a hand though. Many hands make light work!" She winked and shifted her knees. "An' yer better be careful with me china pieces and me cabinet!" I glanced over at her pride and joy, the china cabinet, standing regally like a gilded throne in the corner. Ma collected cups and plates and tea-pots. None of them matched but she said they were special. Bargains found in markets and on second-hand stalls. Ma had a good eye for spotting a bargain; so did Aunty Julia.

"But it's dead heavy, that china cabinet, Ma," Jimmy moaned miserably.

"You and Johnny are strong lads, Jimmy, so stop yer moanin' an' exaggeratin'. I swear yer g'tting more and more like yer Aunty Julia every day, what with all them exaggerations!" She laughed over his head. "Anyway, Monk Murphy is gonna shift the cabinet. I hope to God he's bloody careful with it. An' bloody sober! I'll wipe the floor with him if he drops it." Ma wandered over to the cabinet and stroked it, smiling fondly.

"This cupboard holds our very best stuff," said Ma, proudly. "Gorra keep a close eye on our china. Many round here would give a right eye for one of me best pieces. Oh yes, we've gorra be careful alright, especially if we have a knees-up and that Mary one from Harebell Street brings her rotten feller. He'd rob the eyes out of yer head while you was watchin' him, that one would. God knows what she's doin' with him. He's about as much use as a one-legged man in an arse-kicking contest. He wouldn't know one end of a hammer from the other. Anyway, one day, kids, *all* me china will be yours."

Ma flopped in the easy chair but kept her eye on the china cabinet. I couldn't imagine what I'd do with a load of old cracked plates and cups. Ma fluffed up a pink, puffy cushion on our horse-hair easy chair with the wooden handles. I had no idea why it was called an easy chair, it was the most uncomfortable thing I'd ever sat on. The knitted cushion was one of the only colourful things in a room of mostly brown. But Ma had a spring in her step and a twinkle in her eye.

"Come on you lot!" She sprung up and gathered us into a wrestling heap on the floor. Punch joined in and we rolled about laughing again.

"I'll let you into a little secret before our bommy gets goin'," Ma chucked us a carrot each. "They make yer see in the dark. Get yer teeth around them an into yer gob!" She rubbed her elbows, pulled over the easy chair to face us and sat back down

"It's a bit of an unusual kind of day is today. A one-off, special sort of day. A day I want yer to always remember." She smiled and rolled up a ciggy. "It's not just about hot potatoes, Duck Apple and burning that auld-arse ugly ol' Guy. I know it's great to have a day full of laughs but remember, it's also a day where we can make good memories." Ma took a bite of her own carrot, and a puff on her ciggy. "Memories live in your heart forever you know. An' memories can never be lost." She jumped back up and give Punch the rest of her carrot and had another puff on the ciggy. "Today is about remembering just how blessed we *really* are. We've got each other! We're together! An' look how many kind friends and neighbours we've got! Let's make a promise to always help each other out along the way. That's what matters."

She wandered back to the china cabinet before turning her head. "That means we always take care of family, friends and neighbours, *wherever* we live and no matter *what* Mr Bloody Face-ache Hitler throws at us. Now, let's get crackin'. We've gorra a Bommy to get goin'. An' loads of friggin' apples to eat!"

Ma plunged her hand into a blue porcelain fruit bowl and rolled over three shiny red apples. Punch leapt across the room, grabbed one, and knocked me, Jimmy and Cath smack bang into a stack of washing on the wooden maiden. We burst out laughing when he suddenly lost interest in the apple and ran into the street with a pair of Jimmy's grey socks dangling in his mouth.

By a miracle of the Gods neither the Luftwaffe[6] or the A.R.P. caught wind of our daytime Bommy. A cracking time was had by all. Ma's piano was christened when the adults rolled out a few barrels and sang their bloody hearts out. It picked them up a treat.

Ma taught us a lot that day – she instilled in us qualities and values that would last a life-time. She gave us an unshakeable faith to carry us through the difficult times ahead. We had each other. We had the love of good friends and neighbours. A strong sense of community spirit.

"And love is the only thing that really matters in the end," said Ma. "The world may not always be good to yer, but remember, nothing except love is real," and she smiled, sweetly. "Focus on seeing love and kindness in *everything*. Know that you are complete, exactly as you are." She turned and closed her eyes for a while.

* * * *

[6] The German air-force

Cath, Ma, Johnny and Punch
(the dog), Flinders Street.

Moving into Flinders Street finally put an end to me Ma's gypsy wanderings. Now she was exactly where she wanted to be. She was home. Next door to her beloved sister in a close-knit community who understood the value of service.

"Whatever life throws at you," she told us kids, over and over. "Pick yourself up, dust yourself down, and start all over again. Don't ever forget that everyone can pick up the pieces and be at peace. No matter what or where you are. God never gives you more than you can carry even when it looks like he has."

CHAPTER 4

IS IT TIME TO GO HOME
YET, MISS?

11 November, 1940

"Yer breakfast's on the table, Johnny. Get yer skates on or yer'll be late for school," Ma shouted up the stairs from the back kitchen.

I quickly pulled on my grey woolly jumper. Ma must've stayed up late last night sewing. The big gaping hole in the elbow of my jumper was neatly darned.

Ma's earlier predictions had proved correct – the worst was, indeed, yet to come. As the cruellest years of war took hold, everyday life altered dramatically. Change was forced upon us. We became a nation taught to 'make do and mend' and 'dig for victory'. The brutalities – in Europe, especially – were unparalleled. Life would never be the same again. How could it? Families were separated, deaths ran into the millions. Storms of fear hung in the air.

A life of rations had become the norm but, even though we couldn't get our hands on any chocolate, thank God fish and chips were never rationed. Ma treated us on Friday nights to a portion of vinegary chips from 'Sally's' on Stanley Road. Those Friday night treats helped keep up a good spirit. Some Fridays we even got a fishcake. To this day I can never pass a chippy without remembering those special Fridays amid days filled with terror.

Most of the mothers were bringing up children single-handedly. Yet the women never let anyone feel alone. They kept a close eye on each other. Sisters, cousins, nieces. Friends and neighbours. Women had forged strong bonds and worked together while husbands, fathers, brothers and nephews were called up to fight for freedom. The terraced streets of Liverpool had kept an unwavering spirit. Crippling heartache visited many a house but love, humour and strength shone through. Those dark clouds of despair and the ever-present shadow lurking around unknown corners would see hope clinging on, as we continued to pray that sunshine would, one day, peep through the dark and gloomy skies.

Schools had closed at the beginning of the war, and the children were organized into small groups, going to people's houses for lessons. A large, Victorian house in Great Mersey Street, Kirkdale, not far from the doctor's and dentist's surgeries, became my classroom for a short while. Gradually, though, the schools had re-opened with shortened hours, although some teachers were missing having been enlisted for military service. Gas mask drills were a daily practice.

"I'm on me way, Ma," I was starving!

I flew to the table, the little wooden crucifix nailed to the wall behind me where Ma could spot it first thing in the mornings. My mouth was watering with the smell of burnt toast. Ma made toast *exactly* how I liked it. Burnt black and hot as coal with margarine dripping through until it was soft and mushy. I also had a big bowl of steaming hot porridge on cold mornings. I sat down at the table, three plates set out for us kids. Ma didn't eat breakfast, and I didn't understand why.

The headline caught my eye. I took a big bite of toast and began to read. I liked that Ma used newspaper tablecloths but since the war began the newspapers had shrunk in size to save on ink and paper. Ma only used the fancy tablecloths on special days and every now and again on a Sunday. During the week the best tablecloths were kept clean and safe, locked up in her precious china cabinet.

"Yer the best reader in yer class, Johnny," Ma tussled my sticky up hair and grinned. "Must be all that reading of the shipping news before the bloody war started. I don't half miss keeping an eye on the whereabouts of yer Da's ship in the *Liverpool Echo*, don't you, luv?"

"Yis, Ma," I mumbled with a mouthful of toast – and kept reading.

"Come on Johnny, let's make tracks." Jimmy breezed through the back door with Punch puffing and panting by his side. He dropped his big brown encyclopaedia on to the table and Cath gave Punch a stroke between his ears. Punch dribbled and slobbered, his big wet tongue swiping a lick over Jimmy's boots. Jimmy tutted and groaned, casting a quick eye around the kitchen for an old rag to wipe them clean. He was very particular about his boots. They had to be shiny. He rubbed, buffed and polished them until they were like a mirror. Jimmy and Punch had been out for an early morning walk.

Ma whispered in my ear. "I bet yer he's been trying to get a glimpse of Amy on her way to school, she leaves early for that posh school of hers. Mark my words, Johnny, I'm not as soft in the head as Jimmy thinks I am. I know a thing or two about young love!"

"Yis, Ma," I mumbled. I couldn't for the life of me imagine me Ma being a young girl in love. Poor Punch's paws were taking a hammering

Hand-made 'Steeries' whizzing along the streets.

*Kids from one of the flower streets are showing off
with Punch and Judy puppets in Pansy Street.*

lately. He didn't normally go out walking with our Jimmy. Glimpsing
Jimmy's face I noticed he was all smiles and googly eyed, so I guessed
he must have spotted his lovely Amy. Ma gave me a sly wink.

Punch shuffled over to my chair, staring up at me with exhausted
eyes. He flopped across my feet, sighing, yawning, and rolled flat on
his back with his paws stuck in the air. I rubbed his warm, soft belly.
"Go up to me bed and have a good snooze, lad, while I'm at school."

He dragged himself up the dancers, puffing loudly, his odd ears
hanging low.

"Time to get goin', Johnny, hurry up will yer?" Jimmy beckoned
from halfway out of the back door, his boots shining again. Jimmy
walked the short distance to Daisy Street School with me every day.
Kept a close eye on me always. And though he often yelled at me and
took the mickey out of me sometimes, I knew he would never let me
down. I felt safe with my quiet, clever, big brother. He knew stuff
nobody else did.

Like brothers-in-arms we masterminded great plans for adventures
on our way to school each morning.

"See yer later, Johnny," we waved goodbye at the school gate, and set off to our own classrooms. I would miss Jimmy when he went off to big school soon.

Daisy Street Church of England Primary School for Girls and Boys was sandwiched between the 'Flower Streets' of Kirkdale and contained its own integral swimming baths in the basement. I have no idea who ever used those baths, certainly not any of us kids and I never once clapped eyes on them. The basement was strictly off limits. New housing stands in place of the school today, but of course, the Flower Streets remain.

The bell rang loudly across the school yard just before a silence crept through every class room.

"Line up for assembly, single file, now!" The duty teacher, with a head like a scraggy mop, bellowed through the gap in the glass panelled door. I joined the long stream of kids shuffling through dark corridors like ants marching towards a crust of jammy bread. The smell of beeswax mixed with the sniff of an old Catholic church hit the back of my nose – and something else smelled. It could have been sweaty feet, or mothballs, or the stuff Ma polished her cabinet with.

We took our place for morning prayer. The dirty stone walls were hardly lit by the dull, swinging yellow light, whose glass shade was so full of cobwebs even a spider would get lost. It glared miserably from a long, black chain in the middle of a high ceiling full of cracks. The small windows sat that high up, I wondered how anyone could ever clean them. They were that thick with dust – maybe no-one *had* ever cleaned them. Only a smidge of sunlight squeezed through the biggest window in the top right-hand corner above the mop-headed duty teacher who sat, clutching a huge, black Bible. The gloomy light destroyed my memories of the sunshine outside in the playground. Another round of morning prayers to start the day. We took our seats on the perfectly lined-up rows of uncomfortable wooden chairs that made your back ache.

The headmistress clicked in her heels across the raised wooden stage, an old piano tucked in the corner. A few stifled coughs and shuffling feet broke the silence and the headmistress cleared her throat.

At the same time a bright red yo-yo clattered across the polished wooden floor and stopped right in front of Mop Head. Muffled titters rippled through the hallowed hall. The headmistress tutted. I crammed both sets of knuckles to the back of my mouth and kept my head down.

Her silver-streaked, scraped-back hair sat in a bun on top of a big head. She peered icily over half-moon glasses and flicked an imaginary piece of fluff off her stiff white blouse. I imagined it was starched with sugar and water, like the way Ma did my Da's best and only white shirt, the one with tails as big as myself.

She glared down from those lofty realms with an eye that could easily freeze Hell.

"Whoever owns that blasted toy, stand up now!" She kept both hands on her hips and strode back and forth across the stage. No one stood up.

"If no-one has the courage to own up, the whole lot of you will have no play-time for the rest of the week." She waited and waited, tapping pointy, black shoes. Still no-one stood up.

"Right!" She picked up the prayer book. "Whoever that yo-yo belongs to think very carefully before you make everyone suffer for your mistakes. Take responsibility and own up them."

The groans were loud, so too were loads of shuffling feet. Very slowly the small thin arm and red face of Johnny Penny stood up. Keeping his eyes to the floor he mumbled "I'm sorry Miss, the yo-yo is mine." The headmistress smiled. "Well thank you for being brave enough to own up. Come on up and collect your yo-yo. But keep it safe in your pocket, young man! You've learnt a big lesson today, one we can all learn from. Owning up is always the right thing to do.

Because of your courage you can *all* still have your playtime, including yourself, young man. Now go on, get back to your seat and keep that yo-yo out of my way!" We all blew out a sigh of relief, especially little Johnny Perry. My stomach began to rumble and I remembered the piece of toast Ma had wrapped up in greaseproof paper for playtime. I couldn't wait.

"*Our Father...*" the headmistress intoned.

"*Dear God*," I prayed, "take me home!"

CHAPTER 5

THE ITALIAN JOB

30 November 1940

The door slammed and I easily cleared the two steps in one big leap. Ma spent ages whitening the old grey stone and would have my guts for garters if I so much as left a smudge. Wind blustered down my neck. It felt that chilly, I tightened up my new woolly scarf. Ma had unpicked an old blue jumper of me Da's and knitted up a new scarf for me. It fitted snuggly, twice round me neck. I turned up the collar on my too-thin jacket.

The bottom end of Flinders Street was heaving with screaming kids. Laughing, shouting, squealing. Something peculiar was going on. The rag man was playing an old army song, 'Come to the Canteen Doors', off-key as usual, on his rusty ancient trumpet. A large brown dog, hair matted into spikes, howled in perfect harmony with the out-of-tune rag man.

"Hey, Johnny!" my mate Tommy yelled from the top of the street. "Hurry up, lad, there's a police raid goin' off in Stanley Road!"

I legged it to catch up with my mates.

Dodging two stray cats fighting over a stinky kipper, I let out a curse under my breath. "What's up, Tommy?"

I ignored the wailing racquet of spitting moggies and kept a safe distance. I couldn't quite make out what Tommy was yelling but I soon caught up with the rest of the gang. We charged up Stanley Road, feet pounding, like a herd of wild buffaloes. We flew past the penny bag shop which had fewer and fewer sweets these days. The window was dark, full of empty space and not much else except a few scattered packets of stale broken biscuits so old even a rat would turn its nose up. I'd have done anything for a bag of gob-stoppers.

Crowds of men, a load of old women, gangs of kids, and God knows how many stray cats and dogs hung around on the chipped yellow steps of the library, our Jimmy's second home. I baulked at the sight of the fish shop – cold, black eyes squinted at me every time I passed it. The stink of shrimps turned my belly and I hated it when Ma made me pull the heads and tails off when she was making fish-paste. Mr Jones burst out of his fruit and veg shop, his black-and-white pinny flapping around his face. Mrs Flannegan crashed into me with her new baby's pram. Voices mingled into a soup of raised confusion.

Our gang pulled up tight outside the Grosvenor Cinema. Two massive Black Marias were parked outside Raffos, the Italian ice-cream shop. Blue-clad bobbies with whistles and helmets were all over the show, bundling the whole Italian family into the roaring black cars.

Wails and cries rippled through the crowds. Like statues we stood, shocked and bewildered. Huddling further into the cinema, we watched the scene unfold in crazy confusion. We stared in horror as the Italians disappeared and the Black Marias were just a tiny dot on the distant horizon.

The grown-ups drifted home, morosely, one by one, solemn and subdued. All of them were worried sick about the much-loved Italian family who had become such an integral part of our local, tight-knit community. But the country was now at war with Italy. Thousands of innocent Italians, domiciled in England, were being interned. Us kids had no idea what all that meant, we just knew our Italian friends were being carted off, never to be seen again. Like so many other innocent victims of war they were suddenly uprooted from their homes and businesses, leaving a morbid silence in their wake.

Kids being kids, we couldn't miss an opportunity to explore. The open, empty shop drew us in like iron filings to a magnet. Tony, the bravest and most curious lad in our gang stepped forward first, gazing into the peculiarly silent ice-cream shop. The unlocked door beckoned us with inviting, invisible eyes. It swung open easily. An eerie cloak of mystery slithered inside with tempting, luring teeth. We squeezed past Tony, pushing and egging each other further in, beguiled and mesmerized. Our pink, eager mouths hung open. Drooling and dribbling, curiosity gripped us. Huge square trays and tubs the size of Ma's mop bucket brimmed over with soft, fluffy ice-cream in a kaleidoscope of colours. The sweet smell of raspberry syrup, ripe and tantalizing tickled our nostrils to the point of no return.

Tuppence Ha'penny, the biggest and oldest kid in our gang – nicknamed from birth for being a few shillings short of a pound – suddenly surprised us all, revealing a natural and unexpected flair for organization and leadership.

"Right, you lot," he ordered with a new-found air of mature authority. "Let's get the show on the road, eh? Youngest kids to the front!" he commanded. "Come on! Single file for free ice-cream!"

We jumped to his command and followed our orders precisely.

Tuppence Ha'penny proved as efficient as any officer, handing out little glass dishes and spoons, and suddenly it was a free for all with ice-cream galore. Party time at Raffos, for free!

There wasn't a dollop of ice cream left that day and a few green faces went to bed that night! We never did find out what happened to the Fuccindi family and although it may be a little late in coming, how lovely it would be if someone from that family could receive our thanks for that unexpected ice-cream treat. The kids from Kirkdale who innocently dined on your delicious ice cream will remember you always, Fuccindis, and we thank you from the bottom of our hearts.

"Grazie Mille per la bella gelato!"

CHAPTER 6

CHRISTMAS WITH HITLER: THE BOMBS CAME TUMBLING DOWN

20 December 1940 (Our second Christmas at war)
"Chuck us the red crepe paper please, Jimmy!" The wireless was playing 'Oh, Christmas Tree' yet again – I knew the words off by heart.

Autumn had drifted into early winter. The magic of planning a bloody good Christmas was ringing merrily through Flinders Street and the rest of Kirkdale despite the horrors of War. Daytimes were still long, and sometimes even warm, but the icy night time chill crept through aching bones leaving cobweb patterns of frost on cracked window panes. Chilled air brought goose-pimples up on the backs of bare legs. The cold sweat of fear dripped freely off every worried brow in the country. The threat of bombing ran high on this, the second Christmas of War. The mothers, though, were determined to celebrate Christmas despite the growing worry of bombings which hung darkly in every new moment. Ma especially prayed constantly for a peaceful Christmas.

Our overflowing wooden table in the back kitchen was littered with sticky, homemade glue and sheets of vivid, crinkly crepe paper whose rustling went right through me like chalk scraping on a blackboard. Paperchains grew like multi-coloured pythons, creeping among the clutter. Punch battled with the crinkly lengths of chains, eager to rip them in half. Cath's paper chains were the best by far and she could beat us hands down on any day of the week. She couldn't beat us at fat little snowmen though.

Punch gave me and Jimmy a hand with the decorations. The long white hairs on his tail made a perfect, bristly beard for the Father Christmas perched on Ma's china cabinet. He didn't mind losing the odd hair or two. Not really. Ma beat us all with her newspaper Christmas trees and Chinese lanterns.

The house smelled very slightly of something orangey and exciting. And cloves. Like the oil Ma dabbed in our mouth whenever toothache plagued us. Scooting shadows danced on our walls in the flickering, yellow glow of gaslight that warmed us up far better than any grey blanket which only scratched, and itched, and drove you nuts in the middle of a long night.

"I hope I get a cowboy outfit!" I said to our Jimmy, who was battling with a silver star stuck between his fingers. "Or a pair of roller skates. The ones with the ball bearings inside the wheels. They're the kind that make you go extra fast. That red-haired lad, Frankie McNulty, from Aspinall Street, has got a pair yer know, Jimmy. They don't half go like the clappers down Sandhills."

"Well, I want new tap shoes," said Cath with a wistful look. "Red ones with white ribbon."

Jimmy said nothing, just lifted his eyebrows and concentrated on removing the blasted silver star. Ma was in the parlour where she was supposed to be dozing. Aunty Julia had asked us to make her have a late afternoon kip on the easy chair. Ma didn't sleep well at night, said Aunty Julia.

"*I* want bloody Hitler to kick the bucket for Christmas." Ma woke up and joined us in the kitchen, laughing.

The days raced by until it was less than a week till Christmas Day. I could hardly sleep a wink and ticked off the days on the advent calendar stuck to my bedroom wall with three gold drawing pins borrowed from next door. Cath had made my calendar in school with blobs of white wool for snow, and twigs for Rudolph's antlers.

His nose was a shiny red button found in Ma's old tin, which had once held loose tea leaves all the way from India. The grey elephants on the lid were a bit faded but you could still make out long thick trunks and golden robes draping over wrinkled, rubbery, elephant skin. The ivory tusks looked sharp and dangerous. You could still smell the strong black tea, though it had long since been drunk. "I prefer me usual cuppa," Ma had moaned when she first tasted it and Aunty Julia agreed, though she said the leaves made better readings for fortune-telling.

I looked at my advent calendar and couldn't wait to tick off another day in the morning. Me and Punch dived into bed. *Soon be Christmas Day*, I told Punch. He washed my face and scrambled under the blankets but not before he let out a burp.

Ma came in to say goodnight, and me and Punch snuggled cosily beneath the heavy winter blankets. Ma had picked them up for a song at Great Homer Street Market. We were warm as toast. Ma kissed us goodnight and sat with us for our usual night-time prayer.

My tired eyes fluttered and visions of a cowboy outfit and John Wayne drifted in front of my closed eyes. Punch snored softly and soon I must have joined him because the last thing I remember was the sound of Cath singing 'Silent Nigh' and 'Ave Maria' with me Ma in her bedroom opposite mine.

But something nudged me and Punch out of our slumber. Was it a distant drone I could hear? We bolted upright on the pillow. Punch was wide-eyed and alert, his ears pricked towards the ceiling. He sniffed and twitched his nose and started dragging me out of bed by my sleeve. Was the bed trembling? I stared at it, puzzled. It looked like the bed was shaking. I spun around, scanning the walls and window. Something felt alive in the room, but I couldn't make out what it was. The hairs on Punch's back stood up. The distant, dull drone picked up speed, wailing louder and louder. I clutched my ears and could almost see the walls closing in on me as my advent calendar dropped off the wall, fluttering to the floor, landing upside down. The scream grew louder and louder, and the room filled with the smell of smoke, like gunpowder from a firework. I grabbed Punch by the neck and clutched my candlewick blanket, spinning around, not knowing what to do or where to go.

I sobbed into Punch's head. "Where's me Ma? Where's me Ma? Ma? Ma? *Where are you?*" An eerie kind of stillness flew into the room bringing with it a sense of time running out. For a moment I couldn't move. I couldn't breathe. Some part of me yelled "GET OUT OF THE ROOM! GET OUT! JUST DO IT, JOHNNY!" The taste of fear strangled my throat.

Ma burst through my bedroom door, Cath screaming in her arms. She grabbed my shoulder, pushed Punch in front, and bundled the lot of us towards the stairs. Ma was yelling, "The street's taking a hit, Johnny, get in the shelter now! Hurry Up! Jimmy? Jimmy, where are you?" Jimmy suddenly appeared, running to join us hurrying down the stairs.

Grasping the rusty latch of our cellar *cum* shelter, Ma shoved us all down the old wooden steps. I stumbled and almost fell from top to bottom. I caught a quick glance at the kitchen clock and wondered how much time we had before the bombs rained down. Spiders and cobwebs snagged my hair. I didn't care. I caught my toe on a jagged piece of wood and bit my lip to stifle a cry.

Aunty Julia and her three children charged into our shelter. Gangs of neighbours poured in, too, and Ma and the other mums immediately took charge, making us kids feel safe and comfortable. Ma had made a fire, we had blankets. We had food Ma had set aside, 'just in case'. Biscuits, tins of beans, condensed milk, tea, grease-proofed packets of crackers. Boxes of church candles, matches, blankets, books, feather stuffed pillows. Special dog biscuits for Punch and Judy. Water in empty pale ale bottles, the dogs' blue and white striped bowls. Our gas masks. Ma had thought of everything to make us feel at ease, planning carefully so us kids wouldn't be scared. And we weren't. With help from me Ma, Aunty Julia, and many colourful tales from our neighbours, we very soon almost felt as if we were on a holiday camp. Songs around the fire, huddled beneath blankets, clutching hot mugs of strong tea. Ghost stories to give you the willies. Ma took a risk, dashing up to the kitchen to boil some water, barrelling back down the wooden stairs with a massive tray full of odd chipped cups without handles full of steaming black tea. Even a small bowl of sugar, swapped with Mrs Morris for a lump of red cheese. But the night was long.

Just when we thought peace was close to hand an almighty bang threw us to the ground. The cellar door of our shelter was blown clean off, landing somewhere in the middle of our kitchen. Clouds of dust and plaster rained upon us. Thank God Ma hadn't been in the kitchen making that cuppa.

Sometime during the early hours, all went very quiet and the all clear sound rang out. We blew out long, deep breaths and sighed heavily with relief. We didn't dare move until the A.R.P. warden walked through the hole where our cellar door once stood. He led us silent and solemn through the pitch black, smouldering streets to the warmth and safety of St. Ollie's[7] Catholic Church Hall where emergency evacuation had been frantically set up. No-one slept for what was left of that awful long night. We dreaded the horrors daylight would bring.

A few hours later, we shuffled slowly through Lathom Street – or what was left of it. In a state of shock, we felt like bedraggled lost souls, tortured, weary, and broken. Unable to absorb the devastation, we were herded like terrified sheep, the grim face of the A.R.P. at

[7] St. Alphonsus' Church

the front of our pack. Bewildered adults and terrified children milled about in huddled groups. The air was thick and acrid, and heaps of rubble smouldered everywhere. The burst gas main belched red-hot flames high into the sky. Scattered debris crunched underfoot, smatterings of brick dust blowing in the wind, catching at the back of my open, silent mouth. Blown-out windows fell awkwardly from crumbling walls, still falling apart.

Only unspoken terror broke the silence in this haunted street. So too did sobs of despair. Dark clouds of sorrow and grief engulfed the once lively Lathom Street. I glanced at Cath who was squeezing Jimmy's hand. No more than a sob had her lips since we left the Church Hall. She'd been through such a lot for a little girl, I should have been able to say something to help her. But I was helpless to know the right words.

"Are you okay, Cath?" I put my arm around her shoulder.

She didn't answer, just kept staring blankly ahead. And then I heard her softly whisper, "I'm scared Johnny, really, really scared."

I reached out and took her other hand. "I know you are. We *all* are, Cath, but me and Jimmy – we've got you covered." Jimmy closed his eyes and we both looked down.

"We're right by your side, Cath." We clutched her ice-cold hands tighter. "Me an' Jimmy will *always* look after yer, Cath. Hitler is just trying to frighten us."

She turned and looked up at me, a hint of a smile trying to turn up the corners of her lips "Well, Johnny, he's doing a good job, isn't he?"

I had no words for my little sister. Not yet.

Ma shook her head pitifully. Her hands trembled, clutching her old, well-used rosary beads. "Dear God," she asked out loud. "What kind of evil does something like this? These are just ordinary people. Our friends and neighbours. Living ordinary lives."

Twelve houses were completely gone. Nothing left except grim devastation. Homes flattened to the ground. Remnants of a bedroom sat peculiarly out of place; a child's teddy bear perched on a dust-filled pillow as though it was just any other ordinary night. The tin helmet of a home guard sat split in half, hanging mournfully off a jagged shard of shrapnel.

"Oh Lord Almighty" Ma pleaded. "*How* do we get through Christmas?" She sucked in a long deep breath and puffed out furiously, as though commanding the courage to receive a great revelation. "Get us through this Christmas, God," she wailed pitifully as tears spilled off her chin, splashing on to her deep purple rosary beads. Ma prayed with all her heart on that dreadful day in Lathom Street.

Somehow we *did* get through that Christmas. Our mums made it possible.

The stoic women drew on renewed and strengthened reserves of hope amid despair and vowed wholeheartedly that whatever sadness was visiting the world their children *would* have a special Christmas Day. Come what may. They wouldn't let Hitler to win – he would not take away this one special day from the kids. Not now, not ever.

We faced three terrifying nights of bombs and raids. Our cellar *cum* shelter was a safety net to our neighbours. Our blown-out kitchen door was quickly repaired and replaced with the help of friends and neighbours. By some miracle our street survived that horrifying spate of bombings. Determined, the mothers gave us kids a bloody good Christmas and took the heartache bravely on the chin.

Father Christmas *did* bring me my cowboy outfit. And Cath got her new tap shoes. She strutted around with a smile on her innocent young face, dancing and singing her heart out. And Jimmy lost himself in a pile of new books and a world atlas, so he could discover the exotic places he yearned to see.

It was a Christmas we would never forget.

The now flattened bombsite in Lathom Street turned into a playground for us kids. Ma and the other mothers used to roar down the streets, "Don't you kids go messin' about on that debris. I'm warnin' yer now!" Their warnings went unheard by our selectively deaf young ears and more than a few cuts and scrapes were collected with the shrapnel and bullet shells.

CHAPTER 7

WISH ME LUCK

31 January 1941

I burst into the hall, home from a morning at school and got a whiff of a lovely, oniony smell. Ma had a big pan of scouse on the fire. I stared into the pan like it was the most fascinating thing in the world. Punch flew at me like a bat out of hell.

"Blimey, Punch, take it easy, eh? I've not been gone that long. You'd think yer hadn't seen me for days!"

The bitter aftertaste of the Christmas Blitz had lingered painfully on. It stung like no other wound – raw and septic, impossible to heal. Time moved pitifully slowly, fear never more than a stifled breath away. Warnings of further raids and bombings delivered yet another wave of ice-cold terror crashing through the streets of Liverpool and other cities.

Yelping and howling, Punch smothered me in wet, sloppy kisses. When he'd had enough of a fuss he flounced off down the hall to our open front door. Next door's marmalade moggy strutted past in a world of his own. His sharp green eyes were fixed on the one-legged pigeon busy making a nest in the gutter of the house opposite. The pigeon was clutching a twig at least twice its size. *How do birds do that?* I frowned, puzzled, and not for the first time I pondered on the mystery of birds who are able to carry twice their size in a simple, yellow beak. At that moment, Punch clocked his arch enemy: *that Bloody Cat*! He pumped his legs forward and took off like a rocket. I laughed as the cat pole vaulted off the pavement, hissing and spitting and scarpered up the street. The one-legged pigeon flew out of its nest. I shook my head. Punch wouldn't catch the cat in a month of Sundays, but he liked to show willing! I watched the chase until the cat finally disappeared and Punch came dawdling back, tail between his legs. "Next time, eh Punch?" I laughed and stroked behind his big odd ear. He hung his head low.

Ma and Cath's high-pitched voices floated down the stairs. Me and Punch marched up the dancers to see what the pair of them were up to.

Ma's bedroom door was partly open, and I could see the two of them rummaging about in a battered old suitcase sitting on the bed. *Where did that come from?* I glanced at Punch quizzically. What were they doing with a suitcase?

"What's goin' on, Ma?" I pushed through the door without knocking. "Why've yer got a suitcase, Ma? An why yer puttin' me jumper in it?" I yanked at the woolly sleeve of my blue jumper. Ma grabbed the other one and yanked it straight back.

Cath yelled over me Ma's shoulder. "We're goin' away Johnny, on a long holiday!" She flung herself around and my neck and scragged my hair. "We're goin' somewhere with a funny long name by the sea. AN' I'm takin' me tap shoes!" She twirled and whirled, flouncing back to the bed and tucked her red dance shoes and best pink dress into the suitcase.

"'ang on a minute, Ma! What's our Cath goin' on about? Goin' away? Where are we goin' Ma? and why? What's she on about, Ma?"

"We're goin' somewhere safe, Johnny. Somewhere bloody safe. A place where Hitler's bombs can't get us."

An urgent mass evacuation of children was spreading across Britain: Operation Pied Piper. Around 130,000 people were being evacuated from Merseyside – not just children but pregnant women, young mothers with babies, and disabled adults. The Liverpool Corporation had arranged for children to be moved to the quiet countryside of Cheshire and North Wales, where they would be much safer from bomb attacks. Many children were being evacuated by ship from Liverpool to Canada, South Africa, New Zealand or Australia and many of these evacuees never returned home. However hard it might have been for many parents this was one way to ensure their children would survive, even if Britain was invaded.

Inevitably children reacted differently to this stressful upheaval, some were frightened, and others saw it as a great adventure. Many had not been to the countryside before, nor seen fields or farm animals, and were overwhelmed by their new surroundings. Having arrived at their destination, gas masks slung across their shoulders, the children were chosen by billeters, who often made their choice based on how the child looked and how strong and healthy they seemed. Many were separated from their siblings which was often very traumatic. Some children were not selected at all and were taken from home to home by the organizers who tried to find them places.

Reports were coming in of billeters being shocked by the condition of children from poorer inner-city areas – they were often dirty and ill-dressed. Lice, malnutrition and diseases like impetigo, scabies, and diphtheria were common in densely populated urban areas, but were very rare in the countryside. Experiences varied dramatically and inevitably a lot of it was down to luck. Many children were having a wonderful time, and some refused to leave when the War ended. Some would even go on to choose to be adopted by their billeted parents. Thousands of children ended up living away from Liverpool for several years. In that time they would grow, and became accustomed to being, distant from their parents, so that when the time came, reunited families were practically strangers. Many would eventually return to Merseyside able to speak Welsh fluently, some would forget almost all the English they knew. The most unlucky children would be placed where they were not wanted. They would have a miserable time, fed poor food, forced to live outside and work long hours. It later became clear that there were several cases of physical, mental and sexual abuse.

Mothers were suffering terribly, too. They were missing their children and at the same time were struggling to cope with bomb raids, rationing and the absence, or even death, of their husbands. The government had asked them to pay whatever they could afford towards their children's up-keep. Parents could visit their children but were encouraged not to do so often as this could unsettle them. Consequently, mothers usually knew little about the people who were raising their children.

I repeated my question. Ma's lips tightened in a half-smile but she didn't quite meet my eyes.

"But Ma! Ma!" I couldn't take it in. It was just too much. "How do you know we'll be safe, Ma? Can't we be safe here at home?"

I glanced around Ma's pretty bedroom. The smell of her best and only bottle of scent, Evening in Paris, lingered as it always did. It smelt safe *here* in our little house in Flinders Street. I didn't *want* to leave my home! The silver-framed photograph of my Da stood, smiling, on the chipped dressing table bought in the second-hand parlour shop in Miranda Road, Bootle. Ma said the family lived in the basement, all nine of them, the other rooms rented out, the parlour kept to sell the second-hand furniture.

"But why, Ma? Why? Why do we have to bloody leave?"

"Because I said so, *that's* why. Now come on, son, trust your Ma."

A tear rolled down Ma's cheek and she quickly wiped it away, turning her head towards the wall. I swallowed the lump in my throat and looked back at my Da's picture, where he stood tall and proud. God, I missed my Da, every single day.

"But Ma, how will me Da find us? How will he know where we are? Where are you taking us, Ma?"

I pleated Ma's green candlewick bedspread between my fingers. Cath was happily singing 'In the Mood'. It rattled my cage... *I* certainly wasn't in the mood to be dragged away from my home! I burst into tears. Ma knelt down on her sore knees, took me in her arms and held me tight.

"Come on, Johnny," she smiled, sadly. "It'll all turn out good in the end, just you wait and see. An' there's no need to be worryin' about yer Da finding us. Yer Da will know where we are, and he'll do whatever he can to be with us when we get back. We'll be safe in the countryside luv, he would want that, *and*… I'm bloody well coming with you too!" She threw back her head and grinned. "Leave my kids? Not on yer bloody Aunty Nellie's life!"

Ma was unemployed by this time, her job at the jam factory had ended, as had Aunty Julia's. Unable to find other employment and managing only on Da's weekly allowance from his shipping company, Ma had decided to join us when we were evacuated.

Out of the corner of my eye I noticed a bundle of papers tied up in a faded blue ribbon at the side of the suitcase. I reached over, picking them up.

"What are all these, Ma? I've never seen them before."

Ma took the bundle from my hands and sat on the bed with a sigh. She slowly undid the blue ribbon and a pile of old photographs spilled out on to her bed. She patted the bed and asked me and Cath to sit next to her. She picked out the first of the yellowed photographs. A strange man and lady on what looked like their wedding day looked back at me.

"That's my Mum and Dad luv, your Nannie and Grandad Rowlands. Doesn't Nannie look lovely in her wedding dress?" Ma smiled and stroked the photograph gently. "And look," she picked up another yellowy brown photograph and her face lit up, "here's one of you, Johnny, when you were just a baby! Look at you in your navy-blue pram!" I didn't know I had curly hair when I was a baby. It wasn't curly now.

"An' 'ere, look, 'ere's one of yer Da when he was just a little boy himself."

Me and Cath stared at the old photo. Da in a little boy's sailor suit! Looking just like me! I couldn't imagine my Da as a little boy.

"Oh, yer the spit of your Da, Johnny," Ma smiled and threw me a wink. But her smile quickly disappeared and she bundled up the photographs, placing them neatly in the bottom of the suitcase.

Punch lay on his back by my feet enjoying a tickle on his belly. Suddenly, a terrible thought dawned on me.

"Ma! Ma! What about Punch?" I flung myself to the floor and wrapped my arms around Punch's neck. "Is he coming with us, Ma?" My heart was racing as I clung on to my faithful dog.

"Now don't be daft son. How can a dog go on a bus to Wales?"

"Wales, Ma? Wales?"

"Yis, luv. Anglesey. To a farmhouse, no less!"

Anglesey was a rural island off the mainland's northwest coast known for its beaches and ancient sites. Beaumaris was a small, medieval town within Anglesey. Its thirteenth-century castle with concentric fortifications and moat would come to fascinate me, as did the Beaumaris Gaol with Victorian punishment cells and an original tread wheel. For now, though, I was just worried about my dog.

"But what about Punch Ma? We can't leave our Punch behind! I WON'T LEAVE MY DOG!"

Big sobs choked me. I held tightly to my dear, loving friend. He nuzzled into me, whimpering with his big sad eyes. He knew something was wrong. Tears soaked and matted his warm fur. I felt my heart slowly ripping apart. Our Jimmy came running into the room and threw his arms around my shoulders.

Ma eased onto her knees and sat down with us on the cold, lino floor. She patted Punch. A wistful smile spread across her face and she turned grey as a sheet. Punch's limp, thin tail was tucked sadly under his trembling legs; his puzzled face was forlorn and lost. He looked how I felt.

Ma and Aunty Julia knew how heart-breaking it would be for me to be separated from Punch and so they had already come up with a perfect, if not bizarre story, to put my young mind at ease.

"It'll all be alright, son. I promise yer. Punch will stay with Aunty Julia and her Judy. Yer know Punch thinks the world of Aunty Julia. She'll spoil him rotten. He'll be that stuffed with biscuits by the time we get back he'll be able to sing a duet on his own. And there's something else I haven't told yer, and yer gonna be made up."

I sat up, waiting for Ma to spill the beans.

"Our Punch and Judy have got very important werk to do while we're away, son. Top Jobs for Top Dogs."

"Jobs, Ma? Jobs? For the dogs? What on earth are yer talkin' about, Ma? *Dogs* don't have jobs, Ma!"

"Ahhhh. Well, that's where yer wrong, son. *Our* dogs *have* got jobs." Ma looked smug. "Punch and Judy are gonna be Flinders Street Patrol Dogs. The pair of them must make sure our neighbours are safe. Sniff out the bombs and shrapnel! Make sure the houses are safe too. Punch'll be that busy sniffin' he won't have the bloody time to be missin' us lot. Me and Julia have even knitted Patrol Hats for them. Make sure they're seen in the dark, like. Best Dog Patrol Hats yer'll ever see in yer life, even if I say so meself! Come 'ead, clap yer eyes on the hats me an Aunty Julia have made."

My eyebrows shot up. Dog Patrol Hats? Never heard of such things!

Ma rushed over to the dressing table and whipped out two brightly coloured, woolly hats. Both had a pom-pom on the top the size of an orange.

"Come on, Punch, over 'ere lad, come an' put yer hat on!" called Ma.

Punch dashed over, wagging his tail, knowing he was in for some kind a treat. But a hat? We sat on our knees, waiting to see what Punch looked like in a work hat for dogs. Ma and Aunty Julia and their daft ideas…

We burst out laughing when Punch turned around. He bounded on the bed with a big pink smile, wagging his tail like the clappers!

The bright orange hat was embroidered with the initials 'D.P.'

"Dog Patrol, of course!" Ma pointed out. Punch's odd-sized ears stuck out like two furry, teapot spouts. A big bowed ribbon dangled under his chin. He was made up! He spun on top of the bed showing off, and caught a glimpse of himself in the dressing table mirror.

"Judy's made up with her hat, too." Ma's face was beaming.

"Like a pair of prize ornaments they'll look, eh, Johnny," she hooted.

Jimmy squeezed my shoulder. "Punch *will* be alright, Johnny, trust me Ma, eh? Anyway," he bent closer and whispered in my ear, "I doubt we'll be away for that long, Johnny, yer know what me Ma's like. She can't stand being away from Aunty Julia, it'll drive her nuts! I bet we'll be back next week!"

Our Jimmy made me feel better as only big brothers can.

I went back to Punch who was still showing his hat off to Cath. I heard me Ma whisper to our Jimmy. "Thank God his tears have gone, Jimmy. Yer the best big brother in the world."

And he was.

Street Games are magic.

CHAPTER 8

THE GREEN, GREEN GRASS OF WALES

1 February, 1941

It was an early start. I rubbed away crusted sleep, sticky in the corner of my half-closed eyes. Ma made us dress up in our best clobber.

"Can't have the Welsh Mrs Francis thinkin' we look like somethin' the cat's dragged in, can we, eh?" She wore her best black and white coat, shiny black shoes and even a pair of borrowed, black gloves. "Mrs Francis will think we're dead posh, eh, kids?"

Ma had been able to arrange our host family through the church, prior to our journey to North Wales, so we knew ahead of time who we would be living with. We were to be taken under the motherly wing of Mrs Francis. A widow in her sixties, Mrs Francis had lost her husband in the First World War, and had two sons who were both away serving their country in the Royal Navy. As we'd discover, she was a strong, independent lady, fit as an ox, running a small farm on her own, with only a little labouring help every now and then from a couple of local farmers. She loved company and could gab the hind leg off a donkey which would match us Slaters perfectly!

I didn't care about Mrs Francis or about our appearance, it was far too early, and I just wanted to get back in bed with Punch. The number 28 tram took us into town and we climbed off a little way further down from Lime Street Train Station. A handful of evacuees joined us and we slow marched over to the station, clutching a battered selection of suitcases and gasmasks.

The early morning dawn cast gloomy shadows on thin, unlit lamp-posts dotted over the town. A dull watery sun rose over Liverpool's grey buildings, and over the dirty, grimy towers and commercial buildings surrounded by sandbags in the hope of protection from high explosive bombs. Muffled voices mingled with thumps and bumps as the morning stallholders wheeled wooden handcarts over lumpy cobbles ready to flog their wares for another day. The smell of oranges, apples and pears mixed with cabbages and onions was peculiar but not so unpleasant. The market traders were well wrapped-up. Woolly hand-knitted scarves and hats perched on top of ruddy, weather-beaten complexions. Ladies clad in thick black shawls. A busy, bustling town, preparing for yet another day's trading.

We headed across town towards the bus station. "Gonna be a long, slow ride to Anglesey," Ma warned for the twentieth time. She hurried us over to the bus station. The engines turned over nosily, sounding like twenty roaring dragons to mine and Cath's ears and spewing clouds of thick black smoke and overpowering, cloying fumes. We coughed as foul-tasting smoke caught in the backs of our throats. I struggled to hear Ma's words over the deafening noise. She grabbed us and shoved us towards our chariot into the countryside, weaving through crowds who pushed and shoved. In a rush so as not to miss their own bus, they didn't even notice us kids and shoved us out of the way without a backward glance. Ma soon found our bus and we climbed up the hollow wooden stairs and made a beeline for the front seat with the biggest window.

"I want the window, I want the window!" Our Cath dropped her suitcase in the middle of the crowded aisle. She was determined to grab the front seat first. She sneaked between legs, whooping for joy as she nabbed the best seat. Jimmy struggled to rescue her case and got pushed to the side by a tutting old man with yellow fingers and a ciggy stuck between fat, purple lips.

"Aww, ay, Ma," I whinged. "Why can't *I* have the window seat."

"Because she's a girl and she's the youngest, that's why, Johnny. Anyway, yer should know by now it's always ladies first. What have I been teachin' yer, deaf lugs?"

"Well It's just not fair, Ma," I whined.

"Come on, just sit down and get yerselves sorted out!" Ma blew out a long puff of wind and her eyebrows crossed. "It's going to be a long trip."

"That's the twenty-first time you've told us, Ma," I whispered under my breath. "Start amusing yerselves," she said and plonked herself down on the seat. "I want to be havin' a bit of a snooze."

I sat with Ma behind Jimmy and Cath and inspected the red velvet seats.

"What yer looking for, Johnny? Fleas?" I ignored Ma, I was just feeling the odd material that felt like a brush.

"Stop licking the bloody window, Cath!" Ma yelled, grabbing a white hanky and setting about sterilizing Cath's mouth. Cath pulled away as soon as she clocked Ma spitting into the hanky.

The posh, red Ribble bus slowly pulled out, roaring and belching, still sounding like a dragon.

"They've got dragons in Wales, haven't they Ma?"

"Course they have Johnny. Don't bring one home though, Punch won't be best pleased, son."

"Can *I* have a dragon, Ma?" pleaded Cath. "Can I, Ma? Just a little one, Ma, like a baby dragon? Can I, Ma? Please?"

"Only if yer keep it in Granny Rowlands 'ouse, and look after it yerself."

"Yis Ma, I will Ma. A dragon is bound to love livin' by Scotty Road. I'll keep me eye out for a little red one and squeeze him in me suitcase. He can sleep in there Ma, I'll make him a comfy bed and a pillow."

"Yis, Queen," Ma shoved her gloves inside her only handbag.

"Don't let Punch get his teeth into a dragon, Cath," said Jimmy. "Say it burnt his tongue? How would he eat his dinner with a burnt tongue? Make sure you take the dragon to Granny's house before we go back to ours," Jimmy warned Cath.

"Course I will, I'm not as thick as two short planks, Jimmy!"

A magical Christmas in Blacklers.

"What yer goin' to call yer dragon, Cath?" Jimmy sniggered. But Cath had already turned her back on us. She had a cob on with Jimmy.

The first grudging rays of morning sunlight hovered on the horizon. A shimmering haze danced over Blacklers Department Store, flickering like a golden halo.

"Can we go to the grotto, Ma?"

"Yis, Cath. When it's Christmas, luv."

"Best grotto in the world is Blacklers, Ma."

Blacklers was a large department store on the corner of Elliot Street and Great Charlotte Street in Liverpool's town centre. It was famous for its lavish Christmas grotto and huge rocking horse – Blackie – which is now on display in the museum of Liverpool. The store, which at its peak employed a thousand people, also had connections to the Beatles. George Harrison worked there as an apprentice electrician in 1959. Despite the building being severely damaged in The Blitz of May 1941 the business would survive. Temporary outlets would be created in Bold Street and Church Street and the first part of the new store would open some years later on 29 March 1953. Three decades later, in 1983, the store would be sold on, when all links to the original owners disappeared. It would close its doors forever in April 1988.

"Can yer see up there, Johnny?" Ma pointed over to Bold Street through the window.

"Yis Ma. What about it?"

"There's an old photography shop on the left-hand side, Burrell and Hardman. Its window is crammed with gilded frames of the rich and famous. When we're rich and famous I'm going to get our portraits done in that shop."

"Oooohh," said Cath, eyes wide with surprise.

"They've even photographed Royalty accordin' to yer Aunty Julia but she might have been exaggeratin' again."

"How are we going to be rich and famous, Ma?" I said.

"Oh there's *loads* of things we could do, Johnny." She smiled, and her eyes sparkled.

"Our Cath could dance her way to the top, like Ginger Rogers. She could even end up in London on the stage. An' you? Well you can be a famous footballer Johnny, scoring goals for Everton, and Jimmy can teach Geography all over the world."

"What about you, Ma. What will you be famous for?"

"Oh that's an easy one, Johnny. I'll sing me own songs and play me piano."

"Better get it tuned first!" Jimmy hooted.

"Cheeky bugger!"

"Anyway," Ma went on. "I've sent one of me own songs to the wireless station. Entered a bloody competition I have! I bet yer a tin of tomorrows they'll be playin' me song next week."

"Have yer *really* wrote a song for the wireless, Ma?"

"Oh yis, Cath."

"What's it called, Ma?"

"Oh, Won't You Come On Home, My Sailor Love."

"Aww, that's nice Ma, is it about me Da?"

"It is, Cath, it's all about my Jimmy, luv."

"Aww, that's so lovely, Ma," Cath took hold of Ma's hand.

"Me Da's gonna be made up with a song just for him, Ma."

Cath and Ma got all soppy.

"We all need a dream, luv," Ma whispered to us.

"Do yer know how Bold Street got its name, Ma?" Jimmy interrupted Ma's dreaming.

"How, luv?"

"Well, it was named after Jonas Bold. He was a slave merchant and a big sugar trader as well as a banker. He became the Mayor of Liverpool in 1802."

"How d'yer know all this stuff, Jimmy?" I asked.

"Me encyclopedias, Johnny. Yer wanna read some for yerself."

"See?" said Ma. "Our Jimmy's gonna teach a thing or two, aren't yer Jimmy!"

He smiled and stuck his head back in a book.

We trundled out of Liverpool, crossing over to a foreign land through Chester.

"Why don't yer have a game of 'I Spy', kids? Tell yer what, you start first Cath," Ma sat back and closed her eyes.

The game amused us until my belly started rumbling. I nudged Ma awake.

"Can I have a butty, Ma? Me belly thinks me throat's been cut."

"Yer always starvin' Johnny! 'Ere, lets see what I've got in me bag."

Ma unwrapped a big pile of corned beef and mustard piccalilli butties. The busy towns had long since disappeared and little villages filled the window with pictures like I'd only ever seen in colouring books. The rocking of the bus was soothing. I was warm and cosy. I yawned and snuggled closer to Ma.

"Wake up, kids! We're 'ere! Come on, we're in Wales!"

Bleary-eyed I shot up, shoved my fringe out of my eyes and glanced through the window. Spittle dribbled down my chin.

"Dust yer jumper down, Johnny luv," Ma pointed at the crumbs splattered over my chest. Cath clambered over Jimmy, eager to investigate.

"There might be a dragon waiting for me, Ma," she said hopefully.

"'Ang on a minute," cried Ma. "Let me tidy yer up before Mrs Francis sees yer."

We jumped easily off the bus. Even in the shade of three loaded apple trees, the air was warm, almost like a summer's day. The late afternoon sun shone brightly and everything seemed to glow. I clearly heard the hum and buzz of bees above a babble of excited greetings from the waiting crowds of people.

I clocked her boots first. Huge dirty brown ones covered in mud. Yellow laces snaked halfway up legs clad in dark green trousers. *Trousers? On a woman?* Never in my life had I seen a lady wearing trousers! They looked like a corduroy pair of me Da's that Ma said were always baggy at the knees. I homed in on the size of her feet. I was that busy wondering what size they were I didn't spot Ma whipping out a piece of cardboard from her handbag.

"There you are at last, Mrs Slater. Welcome to Wales!" Her sing song voice snapped me out of my thoughts and the boots came dancing towards us. I glanced up at Ma and saw the piece of cardboard held above her head with 'THE SLATERS', written in black spidery print.

"Oh just call me Emily, luv. Don't want to feel any older than what I am!" laughed Ma.

The big-booted lady's strong arms pulled the four of us into a big hug. Ma whispered to me, "Well, say hello to Mrs Francis, Johnny!"

"*Yakkedy dah!*" I piped up proudly, showing off the only Welsh word I knew. Ma taught us the word but none of us knew what it meant. Not even our Jimmy.

Mrs Francis laughed and clapped my back. She smelled of leather and something I imagined cows must smell of.

"Let's get you up to the farmhouse, its only five minutes up the back track."

We tried to keep up with Mrs Francis's long strides, squelching through thick, brown mud. Trees lined each side of the track, tall and thick.

"You've brought the sun with you Emily, it's almost like a summer's day!"

"Yer can say that again," mumbled Ma, wiping sweat off her forehead. Her best shoes were covered in mud up to her ankles.

"I can't wait to show you the farm!" shouted Mrs Francis. "I've a treat for you in the garden. Might as well make the most of this late sunshine. It's a wonderful winter gift! Over there," she said. "Look, over to the right." Mrs Francis pointed to her farm house.

The house sprang up from hills so green and thick you'd think they were carpeted. It seemed to have lived there forever, weathered by a hundred years of savage storms and blustery, salt-filled winds, swept in off the rolling Irish Sea, and by a hundred baking summers of scorching heat from an unforgiving, burnt orange sun. The thick stone walls were dappled with every kind of grey. Perched on top of the walls sat a glistening blue slate roof sloping low over the top set of four perfectly square, rich- copper windows. Dead center stood a wide wooden door, cast in the same copper hues, at least double the size of our own front door in Flinders Street. From the thick square chimney came the sound of a woodpecker, hammering away on the old copper pot of the smoking chimney.

With the onset of the Second World War, Anglesey had been militarized with three air bases and the influx of thousands of evacuees. But the island's remoteness had not left it untouched. Its geography made it an ideal starting point for monitoring the German U-boat menace that powered the Irish Sea. Around half a dozen airships operated out of Mona airfield to keep a close eye on the activities of the German submersibles. A naval base was also set up for the same purpose. The early introduction of military aviation would go on to shape the future of the island during the Second World War and beyond. The burgeoning conflict had a very profound effect and the legacy of both wars is still felt on Anglesey today. We had, without doubt, stepped into a whole new world.

I gazed at the stony hills, standing silently behind the farmhouse. Spread with clusters of dark, mysterious trees. Rocky outcrops nestled high above waterfalls, streaming like pumping veins.

Sheep stood huddled in clumps, ghost like, silent keepers of the stony hills. The only thing bigger than the granite hills was the pale blue sky sprinkled with puffy white clouds, as endless as any human eye could see.

One small and solitary sheep stood on the edge of a sharp ledge, his stubby tail unmoving, his smallness magnified by the vastness of the hills

"We'll be having homemade lemonade and biscuits on the lawn," said Mrs Francis. "Mustn't waste a single minute of this beautiful day."

"Yer right there Mrs Francis. God knows it could be bloody freezin' tomorra, knowin' our bleedin' luck!" They laughed together and looked up at the sky.

"You must be starving and very thirsty. I've got us a big lamb stew in the oven for supper tonight. Come on, keep up with me."

We struggled further up the muddy track to join her at a wooden gate.

"Well, boys," she said. "Do you think you could milk a cow?"

"Milk a cow?" Jimmy gasped. "We've never even *seen* a cow Mrs Francis, never mind flamin' well milk one!"

"Oh you'll soon get the hang of it. It's your first job in the morning at the crack of dawn!"

Mrs Francis pushed open the wooden gate. She moved gracefully despite her size.

Clumps of mud littered the sloped, stone farmyard. It merged with green fields and from the empty fields the farmhouse rose up in the middle. The smell of something new hung thickly in the air and I pinched my nose. "Manure!" laughed Mrs Francis.

Barns and sheds with rusty, corrugated tin roofs lined one side of the yard. Stables and wire meshed chicken coops were crammed together on the opposite side.

To my left, in two of the ancient barns, two enormous black-and-white cows stuck bristly pink noses over the door. Gentle, blue black eyes with wavy eyelashes fluttered and blinked at us. "Cows are very nosy, Johnny, and very friendly. Go and give Daisy and Bluebell a stroke and a fuss." We didn't need asking twice and legged it over to our new, four-legged friends. Big fat tongues the colour of chewing-gum slobbered and slurped all over our heads.

"*Over here, kids, come and get it!*" Mrs Francis was ready to serve us homemade lemonade and cake on the lawn.

* * * *

The farm in Anglesey was every kid's dream. The big stone house was cozy and loving, warmed as it was by the huge black range in the country kitchen. Every single day, the delicious smell of baking and fresh eggs collected by Cath straight out of the henhouse. The rolling hills and fields were a safe, healthy place to play and explore, to create brand new stories and live our dreams to the full. We were never happier than with muddy boots and the wind tousling our hair.

Freedom. Safety. Peace.

Of course there were chores, but that's how we got to feel important. To know we were needed and worthy.

There was time and space for work and play. A perfect balance.

I learned how to round up the cows. I learned how to churn butter. I learned hay making. And I sat on a three-legged stool and learned how to milk a cow! Mrs Francis even gave me the odd soaking of warm milk straight from the teat. Pistol teats drawn at dawn!

Ma began to fret, though, when she received a letter from the War

Office informing her that my Da would be away for the duration of the War. Ma had desperately hoped and prayed he would somehow be spared from a long service. She began to question her faith and made the decision to return to her Catholic beginnings – a faith she had given up to marry my Da, who was Church of England. Ma's roots in her faith, although it had lapsed, had never truly left her.

Ma took us children to be baptized Catholics in a beautiful church in Anglesey – Our Lady, Star Of The Sea. "There's nothing like a war," said me Ma, "for bringing along a change of heart."

Ma did what she felt was right for the sake of her children. Telling my Da, though, would be a whole different ball game!

"I'll cross that bridge when it comes," said Ma, pulling up her shoulders and straightening her back. "No need to put the cat among the pigeons until I have to, eh Johnny?" She smiled and squeezed my hand.

Aunty Julia kept us up to speed with news of Punch and Judy and the goings on in Kirkdale, in weekly letters from Liverpool.[8]

[8] See Appendix for Julia's letters

CHAPTER 9

DAD'S HOMECOMING

16 April, 1941

The sun streamed through the farmhouse kitchen window. Scraping butter on the still warm cherry loaf not long out of the oven, I shoved in another big chunk.

"Oy, you, leave some for the rest of us!" Mrs Francis swiped the top of my head with a tea towel. She was putting the last of the breakfast dishes away in the tall cupboards. "Oh, go on then Johnny, have another slice. I don't know son, you've got me wrapped around your little finger."

She wandered over to the sink and scraped the leftovers from last night's supper into a big rusty pan. It was my job to lug that heavy pan over to the pig-sty at the furthest end of the yard. The snorting, hairy pigs were always hungry and kicked up a fuss if I was late with their grub.

The kitchen door suddenly flew open and Ma came dancing in. Her wide hips jiggled, as she waved a letter in the air. Her smile lit up the kitchen. "Where's our Jimmy? Where's Cath?"

She flung open the back door and yelled across the farmyard. "Jimmy? Jimmy! Where are you, luv? Cath? Cath! Come inside right now. Come on, hurry up!"

"Cath's in the henhouse, Emily, and Jimmy's probably stuck in a book, hiding in the cowshed. What's the matter, Emily? What on earth's happened? Will you keep still, for goodness sake!" Mrs Francis glanced over at me and shrugged her shoulders

"Here, come and sit down and get your breath back, Emily, before you give the lot of us a bloody heart attack!" Mrs Francis shoved Ma in a chair. Jimmy and Cath came flying through the back door.

"What's the matter, Ma?" Jimmy threw a book on the table and Cath carefully placed a basket full of eggs on the sideboard before she climbed up on the chair next to Ma.

Mrs Francis poured a hot, sweet cup of tea and shoved it into Ma's hand. "It'll settle your nerves, Emily. Now come on, spill the beans. What's all this fuss about?"

Ma waved the letter above her head.

"He's comin' home! He's comin' home! Your da's finally comin' home! Can you believe it?" Tears rolled down Ma's cheeks and laughter got all mixed up with sobs from the lot of us.

"When's he home, Ma? When can we see our Da again?"

Ma and Mrs Francis made the travel arrangements back to Liverpool. By train this time, Mrs Francis said it was quicker. Da would be home for a week, maybe two if we were really lucky. It had been eighteen months since we'd waved him goodbye. It felt like a lifetime. Mrs Francis came to wave us off at the train station and we left with the promise that we would soon return and explore more of the green, green grass of Wales. We stared silently at the large basket of goodies covered with a red gingham cloth and gulped back some tears.

"I can't be sending you all that way home without a few home-baked goodies. Can't have you getting hungry on the long journey back," Mrs Francis wiped away a tear dripping down her rosy cheeks and turned away. "Oh, I am going to miss you."

We hugged her tight. "We'll be back, Mrs Francis, just you wait and see," gulped Ma. "We'll be under yer feet before you know it." We sobbed together as the train pulled up and the guard opened up the doors. It was time to wave goodbye to Wales.

I was like a cat on a hot tin roof all the way home. Dying to see me Da. Dying to see our Punch. I'd missed them both so much. The train dragged slowly, none of us could settle. When we finally turned the corner into Flinders Street our Punch was already bounding up the pavement to greet us. He leapt into my arms, smothering me in sloppy kisses and whines.

"Bloody hell!" shouted Aunty Julia from our front door. "Punch could hear yer comin' a mile off, or smell yer! Have yer been muckin' out or somethin'?" she laughed and ran up to wrap us in her arms, Judy following behind with a wagging tail.

Da was docking in Liverpool the next day. For twenty-four hours we anxiously twiddled our thumbs.

It was early evening when Da finally knocked on the door. Brown as a berry and grinning like a Cheshire cat. Punch went crackers! Jumping, howling, sniffing, licking. We threw ourselves at Da, all speaking at once, desperate to get the most hugs and kisses. And he hadn't even got through the hall!

Ma had been up to her elbows in the kitchen all day long, cooking up Da's favourite meal. A big pan of scouse with a load of red cabbage. Even a home-baked apple pie with custard! And me Ma hated baking!

"The way to a man's heart Johnny, is through his belly," she smiled, wiping flour-covered hands on her pinny.

After our scouse we huddled around the fire, warm and cozy, bellies full. We couldn't stop looking at Da in the easy chair.

Ma clocked the hole in his sock. "'Ere, Jimmy, yer better whip that sock off quick and give it 'ere. I'll get me needle and thread." She rummaged through drawers for her sewing tin. "Can't 'ave yer sittin' there with bloody holes in yer socks! Imagine if one of the neighbours came knockin'? I'd be the talk off the wash-house for a month of Sundays. Come on, give it 'ere, Jimmy." She leaned over and yanked off his sock.

"Awww…eh, Emily! Me feet are gonna get all cold now!"

"Oh stop yer whingin' Jimmy, I'll only be a minute. Do as yer told."

Da winked. He loved Ma fussing over him, really.

Da spent his first evening home regaling us with tales of adventures overseas. Jimmy, never one to miss out on another Geography lesson, lapped up Da's tales about Turkey and Egypt. Cath and I were more interested in the big box of Turkish Delight!

Da showered us with gifts from his huge kit-bag. Sweets galore, bars of chocolate, silk tablecloths and hand blown Egyptian glass ornaments to add to me Ma's growing collection in her china cabinet.

Best of all for me was the unexpected ukulele (and the red fez from Egypt).

Music was always a big part of our family life – we made our own entertainment. Ma sang and played the piano, Da played the harmonica, Cath danced and sang, and Jimmy played the drums with home-made drumsticks and a set of old saucepans. One day, he promised himself, he would have a real drum kit. I'd been itching to learn the guitar, so my ukulele was perfect to get me strumming. Aunty Julia would teach me, she knew a few chords. She was also a great singer and could play the accordion whenever she could get her hands on one.

"Yer know what, lads," Da leant back and stretched out his arms. "When we get rid of bloody Hitler, and we will, I'll take yer to see Germany."

"What about me?" yelled Cath between mouthfuls of Turkish Delight.

Da laughed and scooped her up on his knee. "You, my little dancing queen, will come to Turkey with me. I'll shove yer in me kit bag and smuggle yer on me ship, then yer can eat as many Turkish Delights as yer want."

"Oy, you lot!" Ma interrupted on her way to the kitchen. "Don't be making yerselves sick with all those sweets!"

We laughed and shoved in some more.

"I might as well be talkin' to the wall!" tutted Ma, smiling.

"I tell yer what," said Da, "how about you give us a song, Cath?"

She leapt off his knee, and her eyes lit up.

"An' I'll get me tap shoes for yer, Da. I've learnt a brand new dance."

"I can't wait, luv," Da smiled and whipped out the harmonica in his pocket. "Jimmy son, get yer drum sticks out, and Johnny, get yerself strummin' on that ukulele, lad."

I jumped up at once, grabbing my new instrument.

"Emily," yelled Da. "Sing us a song Ma, before we say goodbye."

* * * *

Many years later, Da described what it felt like, coming home on a short leave during the war.

"It was strange," he said, "being home after so long apart. I still remembered everything about our home and Kirkdale. My easy chair, your Ma's piano. Cath's fancy dancing. You and Jimmy playing instruments that reminded me of laughter and songs and the importance of togetherness. The front door had faded since I last saw it. The paint was chipped and flaking. But I still recognized it. The door that looked like the colour of the sky before a beautiful sunset on a glorious night.

"I walked up to that door, dragging my kit-bag. I raised my hand to knock, but I hesitated. I took a long deep breath and forced myself to rap three times, as I always did. I heard it echo through the hall. I heard your pounding footsteps rushing to open it. I felt it open with a peculiar sense of slow motion. And there you all were. My Emily, my wonderful kids and Punch, because like I've always said, there's no show without Punch! Your warm, loving faces all lit up. I embraced each one of you, my family, in a tight hug that was never-ending in my heart. And I never wanted to leave you ever again.

"But the war still raged on and too soon we once more had to say goodbye. It shredded my heart."

CHAPTER 10

THE EMPTY CHAIR

1 May 1941

Da returned to sea and our house felt empty. It was lonely. Reminders of Da in every corner of our home. His slippers in the hall, his overcoat, heavy with the smell of his tobacco. His cap on the china cabinet. The empty space in his easy chair. We struggled with Da's absence again, with not knowing where his ship was bound. We knew only too well the dangers of sinking ships and German U Boats.

"I tell yer what, kids," said Ma "Let's have one more week here in Liverpool and then get back to Anglesey and see what Mrs Francis is up to on the farm. How does that sound?"

We all agreed and Ma's decision to stay at home an extra week was made. It was one she came to regret.

The warnings of air raids came the very next day. Ma desperately tried to make arrangements and get us back to the safety of Wales but it was impossible. The imminent threat of bombing meant no transport was available.

"Well, kids," puffed Ma. "Looks like we'll just have to sit tight, see what happens and bloody well get on with it." She hugged and reassured us worried kids. And then she smiled. "Anyway," she puffed out another curl of blue smoke from a rolled-up ciggy, "it mightn't be as bad as they're sayin'." She leapt up and smothered us in another hug.

"Come on gang, grab our Punch and let's get to yer Aunty Julia's. We'll have a nice cup of tea and put the world to rights. No use sitting here with faces trippin' us! What will be will be."

Punch wagged his tail at the mention of Aunty Julia and Judy. He knew a few biscuits were likely. Ma grabbed our hands and together we stepped out, ready for whatever Bloody Hitler was about to throw our way.

That very night the May Blitz started, eight sleepless nights when Hitler brought horror to Liverpool. The Luftwaffe wreaked havoc from the skies. The relentless bombardment devastated Liverpool and Bootle, as enemy aircraft terrorized in night time attacks.

Thousands of terrified people fled the city in a desperate bid to reach the safety of the countryside. But just like Ma, many were unable to secure transport to safety. Some people gathered in public shelters; we took refuge in the cellars at home, doing whatever we could to protect ourselves.

For eight terrible nights we lived in fear. And fear can bring out deep facets of our character previously dormant. Within our shelters we found strength and common-unity. We used that strength of spirit to find humour and comfort in dire circumstances. There was no loss of jokes and songs in our cellar, and it kept us going strong.

Ma made it warm, cozy and comforting, kept it stocked with food, drinks, blankets and the wireless. Punch and Judy had their own pile of comforts. Plenty of bones. All sorts of biscuits. Punch never left my side: wrapped up in a candlewick bedspread he kept a close guard on me, Cath and Jimmy, in this strange, new territory.

At times we could even imagine it was a jovial get together.

Mrs Duncan, the pint-sized, barrel-shaped grandmother with silvery hair puffed out her chubby cheeks and chortled, "Bloody hell, Emily, it's like goin' to the pictures comin' to your shelter, luv! Where do I get me ticket? I do hope I've brought me bleedin' snuff."

But certain rules still applied. Even in shelters people slipped into their natural, identifiable roles. Ma was, and always would be, the boss of our cellar!

On the third night of bombing a newcomer challenged Ma's role, to her detriment. She was a tall woman was Mrs Rodgers: a daunting lady of at least six foot two without shoes. Shining auburn hair scraped in a bun at the back of her neck gave her a severe, headmistressy, kind of look. She lived over Jack Webster's Butchers on Stanley Road, not

Ma and Aunty Nellie in Lilly Longshanks' back yard.
Aunty Julia is in the parlour, helping Lilly drag her
pet monkey 'Blinkey' off the curtains.

far from our house. She carried an air of authority which, coupled with her stature, terrified the lot of us. And she was just a few knives short in the cutlery drawer. We christened her Lilly Longshanks. She made her first mistake when she tried to assume leadership on the third night of the Blitz. She rattled Ma's cage. Her long pointy fingers fiddled with the rosary beads clutched in pale white hands as she announced with the importance of a queen: "It is time for prayer. One decade of the rosary. All of you… follow after me."

Our huddled clutch mumbled in hushed but seething tones . Ma leaned over to Aunty Julia. "Where's her blocker, Julia? Comin' in 'ere on her high horse and takin' over! Bloody hell, she isn't even a Catholic!"

"Well, what d'ya expect, Emily," Julia leaned in closer.

"She's a penny short of a pound, luv. I mean to say, who in their right mind keeps a bloody monkey for a pet? Don't get me wrong, Emily, Blinkey's a lovely monkey an' all but can yer imagine the state of her 'ouse? I've clocked those hairy arms swingin' on her curtains. Yer should see the bloody state of them, hangin' down like a sheet of rags. An' it's little wonder the bloody monkey blinks a lot. That woman can't sit still for a minute, poor little fella mustn't know if he's comin' or goin'! An' would yer look at the state of the head on her, she looks like a bloody lodgin' house cat. Yer better knock her off her perch, luv, before she gets her feet under the table."

"Oh I will, Julia, just give me a minute luv, an' I'll get me right head on..."

Day four of the Blitz brought Ma an unexpected visit from a dear friend, Mrs Hardy, who she hadn't seen in several years. She was a kind, gentle lady with a voice as soft as butter. Her two small children had manners to make your heart sing, said Ma.

Ma fussed over her old friend all day. Laughing at their youthful memories over a cup of tea and fruit cake. Her children lent delighted ears to Punch who amused them for hours. He reveled in the giggles of brand new kids he could play with. Ma quickly whipped up a steaming bowl of scouse. Mrs Hardy set the table with our best, unchipped china and mostly matching cutlery. Ma's finest silk tablecloth in green and gold, hand-stitched in Egypt adorned our old table. Our much-used brown tea-pot puffed out a steady stream of hot tea from its chubby spout and sat comforting us from the middle of our table. Ma and Mrs Hardy sat facing each other, eyes and hearts remembering and reflecting on the good times they'd shared. The happy years before the War had torn them apart. A heartfelt dinner marked their deep and lasting friendship.

It was still light when Mrs Hardy unhooked her children's coats and hats off the back of the door. The kids, reluctant to leave the warmth and love received from Punch, complained and didn't want to go.

"We have to be gettin' back to our own shelter. Come on kids, it's a bit of a walk so let's get movin' before it gets too dark." Mrs Hardy turned to Ma raising her eyebrows at the kids' moans and groans. "Why don't yer stay here with us, luv, and use our shelter?" Ma pleaded, but Mrs Hardy was adamant. She wanted to return to her own shelter.

"Me neighbours will only worry and wonder where we've disappeared to, Emily, as much as we'd love to spend the night with you. Another time, eh, Emily?"

Ma couldn't change her mind for love nor money. Neither could her kids. Mrs Hardy had made her mind up and that was that. They waved a tearful goodbye on the doorstep, stifling sobs with promises to meet up tomorrow.

It was a tomorrow that never came.My poor Ma heard the heartbreaking news early the next morning.

Mrs Hardy's shelter had taken a hit. Her long-time friend and those beautiful children were killed outright with everyone else in that shelter. Ma wept buckets for her dear, lost friend. Wracked with guilt, she found it difficult to forgive herself, her inability to persuade her friend to stay with us that fateful night. *"Why? Why couldn't I have made her stay? Why? Why?"* She prayed over her helplessness.

The continuing horror of The May Blitz ran wild through our streets. Hundreds of bombs rained down. Thousands of innocent people were ruthlessly killed. And thousands were left with terrible injuries. One of the worst losses of life happened at the Mill Road infirmary where eighty-five people died. Most were mothers and new-borns. One family lost ten members when their home was bombed. Families torn apart. Families wiped out. It was Liverpool's worst nightmare.

On the eighth night of bombing the all clear siren rang, signaling the end of the Blitz. That siren was music to our ears. We took stock of the dreadful scenes of what was left of Liverpool.

More than 90,000 homes were destroyed over those eight sleepless nights. More than 700 water mains and 80 sewers were damaged. There were more than 500 gas main breaks. The Luftwaffe had dropped over 800 tons of high explosives and more than 112,000 incendiary bombs.75, 000 people were left homeless and bereft. Bodies were placed in temporary mortuaries. It was a double tragedy when the makeshift mortuary in the gym of Marsh Lane baths in

Bootle was bombed out. It prevented 40 unidentified persons from ever being identified and buried individually. Many of those were killed the night before when the Co-Operative store shelter in Stanley Road was also bombed out.

Even in tragedy some wicked people took advantage. It was rare, thank God, but it did happen, appalling and scandalous as that may seem. Like one disgraced undertaker. Well known in Liverpool, he horrified us all when he was discovered to be burying coffins filled with sandbags. It seems he was making false insurance claims, receiving funeral money for sandbag-filled coffins and taking advantage of the terrible loss of so many lives. 'Sandbag Daly' was charged and fined very heavily; he served time in prison for that despicable criminal act.

It didn't seem possible that a broken city could ever pick up the pieces and carry on. But we did. We found strength within our terrible heartache. We picked ourselves up. The clean-up operation began in earnest; Liverpool refused to stay down.

Over two-and-a-half thousand troops and nine thousand workers from outside the city banded together and helped remove tons of debris from the streets. By some miracle we survived the terror of the May Blitz and carried on. *For the sake of our children*, said Ma, time and time again. Everyone lost someone in that awful week. Tragic memories that linger in saddened hearts at quiet moments.

What was left after the Blitz.

CHAPTER 11

BLOODY NONSENSE, SAID MA

1 September, 1941

Posters appeared out of nowhere. Plastered on pub windows, street corners, lamp-posts.

"BEWARE: Secret agents and spies lurk around your every corner…"

"Careless Talk Costs Lives!"

Another poster glared over at me and me Ma from the window of Mulveal's grocery shop on the corner of Rockingham Street. We were collecting our meagre food rations.

Struggling with shopping bags we lugged home our sugar allowance, a small slab of red cheese, a half block of greasy margarine, potatoes and vegetables. We picked up whatever meat was available that week. A packet of tea-leaves and the foul-tasting dried eggs were last on our list and then we could get off home. Ma eked out carefully measured portions to last us until the following week. If the timing was right we could get a jar of jam, issued every two months. The heavy shopping bags dragged on my small wrists and left red welts smarting for days.

Shuffling along Commercial Road more orders screamed out from the walls and Ma frowned again.

"Watch out!" The new poster warned. *"There's a spy about!"*

Warnings to put the fear of God in everyone. There was no escape in the comfort of our own homes either, not with taunts coming through the wireless. Every day a mixture of propaganda and news flowed through the wireless – we were enthralled and revolted by Lord Haw-Haw, the Irish-American William Joyce who fed Nazi propaganda to the UK from Germany.

His broadcasts always began with the announcer's words, "Germany Calling, Germany Calling, Germany Calling!" The broadcasts urged the British people to surrender and were well known for their jeering, sarcastic and menacing tone. Lord Haw-Haw recorded his final broadcast on 30 April, 1945 during the Battle of Berlin. Rambling and audibly drunk he signed off with a final defiant '*Heil Hitler*' and farewell. The next day Radio Hamburg was seized by British forces and Lord Haw-Haw was eventually hanged for treason in January 1946.

Long before this, though, back in 1941, Ma had had enough: "Sod it!" She yelled across the room and scratched the top of her red head. "That bloody Lord Haw-Haw is gettin' on my bleedin' nerves." She threw the pink cushion over to Punch on the easy chair and squeezed in beside him.

"He won't be happy until he's got everyone that scared even a bloody monkey would jump out of a banana tree."

Ma took a long puff on her ciggy. Me, Jimmy and Cath kept our heads down, lying on the floor, reading books and comics. Punch jumped down and joined us, stretching out in front of the fire.

Ma turned her eyes up to the ceiling, drumming her fingers on the wooden arm of the easy chair. She suddenly leapt up. "Me mind's made up!" she declared. "We're goin' back to Anglesey. Tomorrer! Back to Mrs Francis and give her a hand on the farm, eh?" She threw her ciggy in the red flames of our glowing fire.

"Come on then!" Ma waved her arms. "Gerrup the dancers, an' get packin'!"

We legged it upstairs and dragged out our battered suitcases from under Ma's bed.

"Put the wood in the bloody hole!" Ma roared up the stairs. "Where yer born in a barn or what ?" Cath kicked the bedroom door shut and tutted.

Punch helped me pack. Scratching the bottom drawer of Ma's dressing table he sniffed out his Patrol Hat. "He knows he's got his special job to do again," said Cath, tickling his ears. Jimmy glanced over his shoulder, struggling with an armful of books.

I stared over at Punch sprawled out on Ma's bed, his Patrol Hat dangling from his mouth. My heart was heavy knowing I'd have to say goodbye to him again.

Punch bounded off the bed and nudged me, kneeling on the floor.

"Where's me pink tap shoes, Johnny?" shouted Cath. "Aww, Johnny," she murmured, spotting my tears. She stretched her small arms around me and our Punch. "Punch'll be okay Johnny, yer know he will. He's made up doin' that Dog Patrol job. Yer know what he was like the last time we went away, didn't miss us at all!"

Cath rolled her eyes at Punch. "He knows every flippin' word yer say, that dog!"

Jimmy grabbed the suitcase. "Let me get these books in the suitcase before me Ma clocks them. She'll only start moanin' that they're too heavy." He hid his stash underneath Cath's flowered nighties and Ma's thick, woolly cardies.I knew Punch would be fine but not a day would go by without me missing him.

* * * *

The bags were packed, our butties made, and farewells said to our friends and neighbours. Ma had no idea how long we would be away saying only that we would play it by ear. We were still off school and weren't due back until late September in a couple of weeks' time. Jimmy predicted again that we wouldn't be away too long, knowing how Ma missed Aunty Julia too much. "I think Ma just wants a little break before school starts again," he said. I felt better knowing that I wouldn't be away from Punch for too long.

We jumped on the number 28 tram and walked across the busy town centre loaded up with luggage, heading for the train. Lime Street Station was all uphill and I felt the weight of my bags and regretted bringing so much. I did wonder if Jimmy had sneaked some extra books in my suitcase.

Mrs Francis was right. The train was much quicker and far more comfy than the bus. We could easily spread out our little picnic. It was still a long journey, though, and we ticked off the hours by telling jokes, stories, and tucking in to our strawberry jam butties. We couldn't wait to see Mrs Francis and her cosy farm again. My belly couldn't wait for her delicious Sunday morning breakfasts! Fresh eggs and bacon; I could smell them now. I wondered if I could still master the art of milking. It wasn't easy. Mrs Francis kept saying I was improving but I wasn't convinced, not judging by the cows' indignant moos.

The train stopped once more in the mouth of another gloomy tunnel. Plunged into darkness, we groaned.

"Bloody hell!" sighed Ma. "It's like the black hole of Calcutta in 'ere!" The dusty windows started to vibrate and Cath climbed up on to me Ma's knee. "We could've bloody walked to Wales faster!" Ma raked her fingers through Cath's ringlets.

By the time our train finally rumbled into our station it was almost tea-time. We were starving! Climbing up another track, we realized we were well and truly lost.

"Maybe it's this one?" said Ma.

"Yer said that about five tracks ago, Ma!" Jimmy huffed and puffed.

"Don't be exaggeratin' Jimmy." He booted a stone. "I should've let Mrs Francis meet us but I was certain I knew the way," Ma whispered quietly.

"Well yer should know by now what yer like with directions," Jimmy grumbled. "Yer couldn't find yer way out of a paper bag!" I hooted and got myself a clout round the ear. I kept my head down as we rounded yet another lane and the smell of vinegar hit us. We stopped dead in our tracks.

"Let's follow our nose," said Ma. "Surely it's a sign that there's bit of life nearby."

"We 'avent seen a soul for miles, Ma, " Jimmy moaned, and Cath dragged her feet.

"I bet there's somethin' around the corner. I've got a feelin' in me bones."

"*Ma and her feelings!*" I muttered under my breath to Jimmy.

She was right, though. We rounded the corner and were greeted with the welcome sight of a small chippy.

"Who'd put a bloody chippy in the middle of the arse-end of nowhere!" howled Ma, nearly wetting herself. "How do they get any customers?" she spluttered. "Yer bloody chips would be stone cold by the time yer got them home!"

But, in the middle of the arse-end of nowhere, that rusty sign was like a godsend to us lost and starving Scousers.

'Davy Jones, The Best Chippy in Wales', it said.

"Thank God," puffed Ma, plonking down her case to rub her feet. "I hope they know where the bloody farm is. Me poor feet are like a pair of pig's trotters."

"Come on, Ma" rushed Jimmy, grabbing her elbow. "Let's get inside and get some flamin' grub before we fall down a grid!"

"Yer exaggeratin' again, Jimmy," Ma tutted with a twinkle in her eye.

We ordered chips and thanked God that the owner, Davy Jones, gave us directions for a short cut to the farmhouse. We found a perfect spot to eat our chips on the way, further up the sleepy lane. Four fat tree trunks beside a babbling brook made perfect stools. A herd of small white goats in the field opposite trotted towards their side of the fence.

"Waiting for a mouthful of chips," munched me Ma. Stubby grey tails wagged furiously, waiting impatiently. Mrs Francis said goats ate anything. We saved them our leftovers.

"I tell yer what," hooted Ma. "Them goats would give our Punch a run for his money. Bloody gobs on 'em! I don't think them chips touched the side!"

As the goats trotted slowly back up the hill without so much as a backward glance, we lugged our suitcases up to the farm before the sky turned pitch black.

We easily slipped back into the routine of farm life. Days whizzed by and Aunty Julia kept us updated with news from home. The streets of Liverpool were adapting to the changes the Blitz had forced upon the city. Every week the postman would lean his bicycle on the gate post and whistle me over: "Johnny? Johnny! You've got another letter from Liverpool..." I would head for the cow shed and tear open the crumpled white envelope from Aunty Julia, eager to hear all about Punch and the goings-on in Kirkdale.

* * * *

Our short visit back to Anglesey came to an abrupt end when Ma decided, as Jimmy had once again predicted, that she missed Aunty Julia too much. Once more we boarded the train for the long journey back to Liverpool. I was prepared for it to be different – it was the War, after all – but the biggest change awaited me at school.

The German air raids which had caused death and destructions on both sides of the Mersey had reduced many schools to rubble. My own school, Daisy Street, was untouched, but nearby St Alphonsus' Catholic School for girls and boys was flattened. The solution for housing and educating those children was to integrate them into Daisy Street Church of England School.

The classes became much bigger, some up to fifty children. The Catholics and Protestants had different playtimes and dinner-times. I started Daisy Street School as a Protestant but was now a Catholic, following my Ma's decision to convert us in Anglesey. Though many of my old friends now had different classes and playtimes we still met up after school and made new friends, too. Separate classes would stay in force at Daisy Street School until the 1960s.

Every day, as soon as the home time bell rang, me and my school mates gathered outside the gates. Ready for a new adventure, we'd leg it up to our house in Flinders Street, pick up Punch who came everywhere with us, then scarper off to muck around on the bomb sites, searching for shrapnel, incendiaries, bomb cases and bullets. All of us on the look-out for the best bit of treasure to show off with.

"Don't yer be goin' anywhere near those bomb sites, Johnny. I'm warnin' yer. Are yer listenin' to me?" None of us kids took heed of our mothers' warnings.

Sweets were rare but sometimes one of us would come across the odd one or two and we'd pass around a half-sucked gob-stopper, three sucks each. Sometimes we even had a half bite each of a liquorice stick. I'd save my bite for Punch who went nuts for a bit of liquorice.

Exploring through the streets of Kirkdale one night, we stumbled across a German landmine at the top of Sandhills Lane. Leaning precariously beside a half-demolished house, the landmine was enormous. We had no idea if it had been diffused or not but that didn't enter our heads. We were that made up to be able to brag about our latest 'find'. We didn't give a hoot, or even think, about the possible danger. (Thank God it had been diffused, much to me Ma's relief when she found out!) The only downside of our miracle discovery that night was the stink of the nearby canal clinging to our clothes.

We drifted further along the streets hoping to find another landmine but when we got to Lightbody Street we came across an even greater discovery. The full fuselage of a German aircraft bomber lay in a tangled heap in the middle of the street. Lying there hopeless and wingless. The stony-faced bobby on guard wouldn't let us climb aboard no matter how many times we pleaded. "Bugger off home before yer see the back of me hand" he yelled, and we scarped quick when he ran at us with his whistle hovering by his fat red lips. But what a great adventure that night turned out to be – it gave us great tales to brag about in school the next morning. Rich pickings for us Kirkdale kids.

Me and Punch dawdled home with more than just a pocketful of memories and a handful of bullet cases. Black as coal but content as a cat, ready for another clout around the ear off me Ma!

* * * *

We didn't think it could be possible, but as the War raged on it reached even greater, terrible heights. On December 7, 1941 Japan exploded into war at Pearl Harbour and America, the sleeping giant, woke up. All hell broke out – yet nobody saw it coming.

The anchored ships of almost half the U.S. Naval fleet sat like sitting ducks on that sleepy Sunday morning. They were either bombed or torpedoed. The U.S. was taken completely by surprise and the aftermath of Japan's act of infamy was devastating. America declared war on Japan; Germany declared war on America; Britain was at war with Japan.

We had entered into the realms of a world gripped by war and fear.

The evil, unquenchable need for power and control raged through North Africa, Russia and the Far East. Those exotic lands seemed so distant and unreal in my childish eyes as I sat in my classroom, drifting and dreaming in blissful, naïve innocence.

CHAPTER 12

A HEAD FULL OF MOVIES

15 April, 1942

Mrs O'Neil droned on and on about the virtues of knowing our times tables. I glanced up at the clock in the classroom: another hour. I sat and twiddled my thumbs. I couldn't wait to get back down to the bomb site with Punch and me mates. We might find some more ack-acks tonight, my collection was growing, soon I'd have enough to do a 'swapsie'[9] with the lads in Lemon Street, see what kind of a stash they had on offer. I hoped it didn't piddle down with rain like last night. I clocked the view out of the window while Mrs O'Neil had her back turned. The sky was a bit grey and looked dodgy.

The new girl, Debbie, sat in front of me, scratching her long black plaits like a dog with fleas. Her blue ribbon had come loose and was dangling halfway down her dirty cardigan. The hole in it by her neck, where the label stuck out, was even bigger than this morning. *I hope she hasn't got a headful of nits*, I worried, *the way she's swinging those plaits around*. I pushed my chair further back. She was alright Debbie, I suppose, but she didn't half talk the hind leg off a donkey. And yer couldn't understand a word she said, whistling with no front teeth in her head. *A head that might be full of nits,* I remembered, and shuffled my chair further back.

Three soft taps on the door interrupted my dreaming. Sister Gonzalga stepped in so quietly you'd think she bloody well floated. We stood up at once.

"Good afternoon, Sister Gonzalga," we blurted out, and Tommy in the front row knocked over his chair again. He was a bit hopeless

---

9 Swapping one item for another

like that, was Tommy, all arms and legs. He was a bit shy too. He Swapping one item for another stood there with a face as red as a turkey-cock. *Clumsy clot*, me Ma and Aunty Julia called him. We stifled a titter.

Mrs O'Neil gave Tommy daggers but Sister Gonzalga just smiled. She was nice like that, was Sister Gonzalga. My favourite nun of all. I wasn't even scared of her black habit anymore. But I did wonder what kind of hair she had and what size shoe she wore. They looked unusually small in those black, flat boots.

"Time for today's Catechism, children," echoed Sister Gonzalga's sweet voice. "Please sit down and bring out your Catechisms." Desk lids clattered and banged. "*Quietly!*" demanded Sister Gonzalga. We twisted uneasily on our seats. Clutching dog-eared little blue books in our hands, the class became silent.

I swallowed hard, eyes squeezed shut. *Please don't pick me, please don't pick me, please don't pick me* went the mantra in my head. Sister Gonzalga chose one child in every lesson. The chosen one would have to answer questions on the Catechism while stood in front of the whole class, without the Catechism to find the answers. She picked me out last week and what a mess I made of that. My face was red all day.

I hid behind my desk lid hoping she wouldn't notice me. "Put your lid down Johnny, please." *Blast!* She'd clocked me. Still, I kept my eyes down and tightly closed.

"Tony Matthews!" she called out. "Come to the front please. Leave your Catechism on top of your desk. Stand next to me till we're ready, Tony." You could hear the collective sigh of relief. *It'll be a doddle for Tony, what with him going to mass at St Johns every day with his Ma, he's bound to know all the answers. And he is a bit of a big-headed know-it-all.*

First came the part were the whole class had to answer, but at least we could look for the answers in our blue Catechisms.

"Who made you?" Sister Gonzaga led the way.

"*God made me,*" we chorused together.

"What else did God make?"

"*God made all things.*"

"Why did God make you and all things?"

"*For his own Glory.*"

"What is God?"

"*God is spirit and not a body like men.*"

"What did God give Adam and Eve?"

"*He gave them souls that could never die.*"

At last we finished and it was Tony's turn for Sister Gonzaga's grilling of the Catechism. Tony did have all the right answers though. I knew he would! I didn't think it was fair, really. I mean Sister only asked Tony three easy questions! She asked me about ten last week, and dead hard ones too! No, not fair at all. Tony went back to his desk strutting like a peacock.

Sister Gonzaga packed up her black doctor's bag and clutched the heavy Bible under her arm.

"Good afternoon and goodbye children. Peace be with you."

"*And also with you, Sister Gonzaga, thank you for our lesson.*" She floated out and those black boots seemed to hover mid-air, leaving a soft breeze as you would imagine an Angel does.

We leant back and blew out our cheeks. *Thank God that's over for another week.*

Mrs O'Neil returned and we moved on to spellings. I glanced up at the clock again. I was good at spelling so I didn't really need to listen. Might as well get back to my drifting and dreaming, that's what I liked to do best. Resting my head on my elbow I drifted away.

I dreamt about the peace Sister Gonzaga went on about all the time. What exactly is peace? I couldn't get my head around why the world was at war instead of living in the peace Sister Gonzaga said was so magnificent – that was how God had planned us to live our

Our local picture house known as the 'Flea-Pit'.
Movies on the screen as well as in my head!

life in the first place. Why did we get it all mixed up then? What went wrong? It's all so stupid and sad. Me Da wouldn't have had to leave us if the world was living in peace. It didn't make sense. *It's a pity life isn't more like the movies, I dreamed. Nice and simple. I mean nobody really gets hurt in the movies. Not for real. It's all only make believe. So why can't life be make believe? Or is it?* I puzzled and pondered, searching for an answer. I wondered if real life was really just a movie after all but we've just forgotten that we've made it up? That got me thinking even more. If life was really just a movie then why don't I change it? Make up a new movie? The whole world could watch it, better yet, everyone could act in it! Imagine! Everyone playing a whole new part. You would be able to do and see anything you want in my movie. Best of all, everyone would be happy and free to choose who they wanted to be and there would be no more war. That's it! That's what peace is! The freedom to play and see whatever you want. That's what I'm going to do! I'm going to make the best movie ever.

I whipped out what was supposed to be my spelling book, grabbed a pencil, and started writing a new movie script for the world.

There would be no baddies. Hitler wouldn't exist. Neither would Mussolini or The Big Fizz as Churchill calls him on account of being all gas and no wind. No Tojo, the Japanese leader either. There would be no war, ever. Best of all our dads would never have to leave their family ever again.

The bell rang loud across the classroom. I flew out of the door, ready to pick up Punch and head off down to the bomb-site, my movie script for a brand-new world tucked safely in my pocket.

I hurtled down Flinders Street like a bat out of hell. "Punch? Punch!" I yelled through our open front door. "Come 'ead, lad, it's time for yer walk!" It wasn't piddling down but the sky was still a bit grey. Punch hated rain. And hailstones. He didn't like snow either. Anything wet sent him hiding under the easy chair. I hopped up and down waiting for him to stop my knees turning blue.

"The cold gives yer chilblains," me Ma said when sores flared up on my feet and knees. "Keep yer feet and legs warm, Johnny," she warned me every day of winter. I stuck my frozen fingers under me armpits. Punch galloped like the clappers down our hall, howling like a bloodhound. He took a flying leap and completely missed the doorstep. Desperate to wash my face we both went arse over tit.

"Alright, Punch!" I scrambled back onto my feet. "We're goin' now, Punch, steady on, lad."

"Johnny! Johnny! 'Ang on a minute, son, I want yer to go on a message!"

Blast! Ma had come scuttling to the door and collared me. "Awww… eh, Ma! I wanna see me mates! Can't our Jimmy go? It's not fair, Ma."

"An' neither is the hair on me head so it makes no odds. Jimmy's at the library stuck in a book. It'll only take yer a minute, luv." She dangled a string bag of oranges.

"Whip these up to Mary Hannah in Brisbane Street, will yer luv? God help her, son, she's got a terrible chesty cough. Barkin' like a dog she is. An' tell her I'll be up after with some kaolin and lint. It'll shift the cough, Johnny. Can't beat a nice hot poultice."

I grabbed the oranges and me and our Punch went leggin' it off.

We dashed through our entry, taking a short cut. Our Cath and her mate Joan were playing two balls on next doors back wall.

"One potato, two potato," Cath sang and bounced the ball under her leg. On the third potato Punch leap up, grabbed her best red ball and went flying out of the entry. "Awww… eh, Johnny!" whinged Cath "I'm tellin' me Ma on you, soft lad. Get me ball back! Yer always lettin' Punch pinch me ball!"

I laughed over my shoulder. When I caught up with Punch on the bomb-site in Rockingham Street, I nabbed Cath's ball and stuffed it in my pocket. One of the lads in our gang, Frankie, was sliding down the banister jutting out between two half walls of what was once a house.

"Are yer coming up to our den, Johnny?" he yelled from halfway down the bannister, his two skinny legs wide in the air. "I'll be there in ten minutes or so, Frankie, I'm just goin' on a message fer me Ma. Meet yer up there, lad. An' watch that wall Frankie, it's leaning to the left."

His Ma's going to go nuts, I told Punch. *She'll batter him if she clocks him on that slide again.*

Punch ran far ahead and I had to leg it fast to catch him up. He was leading me his own way. We ended up going all the way round the houses before we stumbled into Pluto Street. "I bet yer I catch our Jimmy down 'ere, Punch. Bet yer he's not been the flamin' library at all. He'll be chasin' after that Amy one, she lives down here, Punch. I'll make a holy show of him if I clap me eyes on him."

Bombo Mac come running out of his house. "Hiya Johnny, are yer goin' ter the den?" We stopped while Bombo gave Punch a good old fuss.

"Just droppin' something off first for me Ma, Bombo. Come with us if yer like and we'll go to our den together."

"Yer on, lad," said Bombo. The three of us took off.

We bumped into a bunch of girls from school playing in Lemon Street. Renee and May were doing handstands by the pawn shop.

"Oy, you two," shouted Bombo. "I can see yer navy knickers!"

Bombo was in stitches. Renee and May give us looks to turn the milk, and tucked matching yellow dresses into knicker legs. Mary was swinging on the lamp post and the rope looked frayed and dodgy. Sadie was pushing an old doll's pram with only two wheels. Lenny had robbed the other pair when we made our go-cart. Sadie didn't know it was us or she'd have wiped the floor with us.

"Hurry up, Bombo," I whispered, "let's get out of here before they collar us for a cissy girl game. They'll only make us turn that bloody skippin' rope again."

We scarpered! Punch first.

They were all at the den. Waiting. Something was happening; all of me mates were huddled in a tight circle. Eddie clocked us first. He came sprinting over with a large piece of shrapnel tucked under his arm. "Johnny! Johnny! Bombo!" he yelled like a foghorn. "Have yer heard the news, lads?" We shook our heads, running faster to close the gap.

"Yer never gonna believe it!" croaked Eddie.

"What? What? What won't we believe, Eddie?"

"Guess who's coming to Liverpool, tomorra?"

We barged into the huddle to hear more.

'Deep In The Heart Of Texas' blasted out of the barber shop's window around the corner.

CHAPTER 13

THE YANKS, AND MORE, ARE COMING

16 April, 1942

We met up the next morning, early. Far too excited to sleep in late. The whole gang of us gathered on Flinders Street corner, anxiously twiddling our thumbs. Punch too, wondering what all the fuss and noise was about. Well, as me Da always said, there's no show without Punch! We couldn't let him miss out on welcoming the G.I.s. None of us had ever seen a real-life Yank before. Only in the movies.

The first Americans had arrived in England in January 1942, "Over-paid, oversexed and over here" as the gripe went, but not so for us in Liverpool, we couldn't wait for the G.I.s to arrive. American servicemen were stationed from one end of Britain to the other. Sent in advance of the planned invasion of Europe. They were more than willing to join in the fight against the evil of Hitler. Sailors, soldiers and airmen arrived in convoys of thousands. Ferried over the Atlantic in the droves. They arrived with full pockets and bellies, something we hadn't seen for a long time. They shared an abundance of all manner of things to boost our flagging morale. The British had staved off the Germans almost single-handedly for more than two years and now the influx of American troops was to be met in Liverpool with welcome relief, and more than a smattering of curiosity.

We poured along the streets of Kirkdale, mingling with the huge crowds all the way up to Lime Street Station about three miles away. Adults, kids and more than a handful of dogs swarmed as one while the khaki trucks and jeeps roared in the distance, the smell of burning rubber mixing with engine smoke and fried bacon.

"What the bloody hell is that?" shouted me Bombo. He pointed to a monster machine with a clawed yellow bucket looming ahead.

"God knows," I said. "Look at the bloody size of it, and clock that massive mouth!"

"That's a bulldozer, lad," smirked Mr Cooper from Aspinall Street. His teeth were yellow and broken like the Ten Commandments. They wobbled in his smug, know-it-all face. His tatty, over-coated shoulders shrugged like we should have known it was a bulldozer. We turned away. The Yanks streamed out: G.I.s, tall and broad. Giants clad in boots of a size I couldn't imagine. We followed the handsome G.I.s like sheep behind a gang of shepherds. Clunky boots marched heavily in perfect time. It could've almost been a khaki green wave rolling in from the River Mersey, riding along with a convey of spluttering engines. Crowds poured all over the G.I.s, dishing out hundreds of cups of tea and food.

The noise was deafening. Horns blaring, screams, shrieks, cheers. I didn't know which was louder, the screeching engines or hundreds of voices. Everyone was either talking, laughing or hollering. Music blasted through the streets, different songs all mixed together. People cheered and whooped, waving hands in a sea of floating G.I.s. Flaying arms grabbed for a quick touch of sweaty, American sleeves.

We followed the troops all the way along Stanley Road. Dolled-up ladies in high heels and lipstick offered cakes, butties, and pies. Women draped over the soldier's thick necks – the soldiers smiled sweetly while their handsome cheeks were plastered in kisses, mouth-shaped splodges streaked across beaming faces full of snow-white teeth. Plates and dishes and boxes of sponge cake, spotted dick, apple pie, and meat paste butties were passed around the enormous crowd.

"Hey Lenny," I yelled. "Don't they sound just like John Wayne?" I flashed a grin at my mate who was craning his neck on top of his Uncle Tommy's shoulders. His Uncle Tommy was that little when it rained he was the last to know: Lenny didn't have much of a view. "Now ain't that the truth," said Lenny, wobbling back to the ground. "It's like we're in the movies, Lenny!" I laughed.

"Sure are, Johnny, sure are!" Lenny winked and drawled in his best Yankee voice. We swaggered behind the Yanks, buckarooing like a couple of brash gun-slingers.

The jeeps drew up on the corner of Derby Road by the docks and set up camp. There once stood a massive timber yard on this spot but now the land stood stark and barren. The Blitz had claimed the timber yard, now burnt to the ground. It was a terrible night when the timber yard blew to pieces. We had explored the damage the next morning. Burning and still smouldering, the timber yard and warehouses along the dockside weren't recognizable, burnt out to nothing or in a state of collapse. Walls still crumbled in front of us. Rubble, dust, muck, bits of old iron, all kinds of rubbish strewn everywhere. Gutters spilled over with foul, dirty stinking water. The gassy smell of melting rubber and charcoaled wood made us cough and splutter on the day we explored. The pong of burnt peanuts, brown sugar, and coconut mixed together like a strange soup, stores of food from the many warehouses. A combined smell of tragedy, once smelt never forgotten. It would haunt me forever.

The blaring horns of the Yanks jeeps snapped me out of my memories. I don't know who jumped highest, me or Lenny, but we shifted out of the way of jeeps and trucks rolling over the land which once lay claim to being Liverpool's biggest timber yard.

The khaki tents sprung up in next to no time. A handsome G.I. the size of a lamp post ambled over to our gang. We stood silent, as if the cat had got our tongues. He carried a whopping big can of something with an orange label. He smiled over and thrust his plate sized hand at me and drawled, "Howdy, y'all little guys. Would ya be having any big sisters now?" We shook our heads and didn't have a clue what he was on about.

He threw back his head and laughed, just like John Wayne. "Grab a peach each, chums." He passed around his big can.

"Peaches!" we gasped. "Wow! Never tasted anything like them before! Thanks, Mister!" I drooled and shoved the peach in my mouth.

He swaggered back to put more tents up but drawled over his shoulder. "Don't y'all be forgettin' now, bring us up yer pretty gals. Ya hear me, chums?" We nodded, too busy sucking on the peach slices.

We went every night after school to see our new American mates. The G.I.s were made up with Punch and called him their adopted Liverpool Mascot.

"Doing his doggy bit for the war effort," the G.I.s drawled.

"He's a war hero, that dog of yours, Johnny. He should really get a medal," said the big Officer who was the boss of everyone. Punch ruled the camp like a dog with four bollocks, he grinned.

They were the best of guys, those G.I.s. We never once got fed up chewing on their packs of chewy. Or scoffing dozens of Lifesavers which tasted like polo fruits. On a good night we even got one of those huge tins of peaches to take home. Me Ma was made up when that happened.

Even better was the super-size comics like *Superman*, *Cape Marvel*, *Cape Marvel Jnr* and *Batman*. Saturday mornings in our den soon morphed into Comic Swappsie Day.

The Secret Password into our Den?

"*Got any gum, chum?*"

A lot of those G.I.s were probably shipped overseas and never returned home. We had much to thank them for, including their offspring. I'm betting there were plenty of those!

It was around this time that me Ma took a job with G.B.E. a, subsidiary of American General Motors, who were assembling American trucks shipped over in crates and put back together over here. Me Ma was made up to be a mechanic, and she could turn her hand to anything. Nothing ever daunted me Ma.

Ma (seated centre) with St Ollie's Mothers Union.

She wore a green boiler suit with huge pockets for spanners and wrenches. I still couldn't get my head around women wearing trousers, especially Ma! The demand for trucks for the war effort was huge and the country relied on women like Ma to take on new roles as well as their usual demands.

"We all have to do our bit for the country, Johnny luv. Everyone can pitch in and do their best," she said.

But Ma made sure she was always home for our dinner and I loved knowing she was there, in the kitchen, cooking something lovely for us. Making tasty something out of nothing. A warm smell always welcomed me home each night.

Friday nights were the best though. Fridays have remained my favourite night of the week ever since. It was chippy night, you see. On her way home from work with her wages, me Ma called in at Sally's Chippy at the top of Reading Street.

"Only the best chippy for us Johnny, luv," Ma smiled and winked. "On the best night of the week. Yer can't beat a bloody good Friday,

Sometimes we would get a meat treat from
Nixons factory in this little street.

can yer, son? Come on, get the bread buttered and the pan on to boil, I'm bloody starvin'!"

"Me too Ma, me too!"

Like me Ma said, Fridays were the best bloody night of the week.

* * * *

The second half of 1942 saw a reversal of German fortunes. British forces under Montgomery gained the initiative in North Africa at El Alamein, and Russian forces counterattacked at Stalingrad. The news of mass murders of Jewish people by the Nazis reached the Allies, and the U.S. pledged to avenge these crimes.

CHAPTER 14

THE TIDE TURNS SLOWLY

1 April, 1943
The sun beat down ruthless and unforgiving, the best spring weather in years, hotter than Egypt, some said. It glistened off the misshapen heaps of shiny shrapnel. And while the unusual heat blistered the back of my neck, peculiar humps erupted across our bomb-site den. *Like mole hills*, I laughed; well, that's what they looked like to me but really the only mole hill I'd ever seen was in the *Beano*. I sweated cobs over my little hump of stash. I glanced over at Bombo for a sly peek of his. His pile was bigger than mine but that didn't mean it was better. Eddie's pile looked rubbish.

"Ten minutes left!" shouted Marty, holding up his Grandad's fob watch.

February had seen the German surrender at Stalingrad: the first major defeat of Hitler's armies. Battles continued to rage in the Atlantic. A four-day period in March saw 27 merchant vessels sunk by German U-Boats. We feared every day for our Da's safety at sea. Later, in mid-May, German and Italian forces in North Africa would surrender to the Allies, who used Tunisia as a springboard to invade Sicily in July. By the end of May Mussolini would fall, and in September the Italians would surrender to the Allies, prompting a German invasion into North Italy. Mussolini would be audaciously rescued by a German task force, led by Otto Skorzeny, and established a Fascist republic in the North. German troops also engaged the Allies in the South. The fight through Italy was to prove slow and costly.

Later in that same summer, in the Pacific, US forces would overcome the Japanese at Guadalcanal, and British and Indian troops would begin their guerrilla campaign in Burma. American progress continued in the Aleutian Islands, New Guinea and the Solomon Islands. As the Russian advance on the Eastern front gathered pace, recapturing Kharkov and Kiev from Germany, Allied bombers would eventually begin to attack German cities in unforgiving daylight air raids. The opening of the Second front in Europe, long discussed and always postponed, would finally be prepared for the following year.

Meanwhile, those in Liverpool were seeing the first glimmer of hope.

Nearly four years of war had left many thousands dead, injured and homeless. Large areas of the city and dockland had been left in ruins. The war had helped create a remarkable unity among the British people and there was a strong feeling that the British should be rewarded for their sacrifice and resolution. To encourage people to continue their fight against the Axis powers, the government promised reforms that would create a more equal society. In December of the previous year Sir William Beveridge, the British Economist, had published a report, instilling hope to hundreds of thousands at home and at the Front with plans for making a better world. A world that would deal with what he called the 'Five Great Evils': squalor, ignorance, want, idleness, and disease – by, among other things, creating a National Health Service. He proposed that all people of working age should pay a weekly contribution. In return, benefits would be paid to people who were sick, unemployed, retired or widowed. Beveridge argued that this system would provide a minimum standard of living "below which no-one should be allowed to fall". The Wartime Education Minister would soon be creating a new education system and would raise the school leaving age to fifteen. People all over Britain and in the shadowy streets of Kirkdale clung on to the newfound hope that the great 'afterwards' was on its way.

Meanwhile, however, at the bombsite: "Come on Punch, keep diggin' lad. I know yer can do it!" He kicked dirt in my face.

"Ten minutes to claim the prize, lads!" Marty bellowed louder, waving his homemade, cardboard megaphone. Only ten minutes left.

"We've just got to find the biggest piece of shrapnel, Punch. Get stuck in lad, keep goin'!"

His paws scrabbled like mad; so did my hands.

"Five minutes!" Marty yelled, strolling past us like he'd just stepped out of the council offices and inspecting us with an air of officialdom. His keen eyes watched the clock. "Three minutes left!"

"Come on Punch! Three minutes to get the badge of honour. Dig deeper Punch, dig deeper!" My knees scraped on the rubble and two of my fingers bled into sandy muck. We shifted a load more dirt. And there it was! He'd found it! The biggest bit of shrapnel you'd ever seen in yer life! I knew he'd find it.

"Yer've done it Punch! Yer've done it! No-ones gonna have a bigger piece of shrapnel than this bloody cracker!" His tail went twenty to the dozen. I flung my arms around him. "Yer the best in the world, Punch. I bet yer we win, lad."

Punch took a fit of sneezing, spitting brick dust in my face. I laughed, wiping sweat and dirt on my sleeve.

"Time's up!" Marty called a halt to our street's Competition of the Year (Who's Gonna Win the Prize for Finding the Biggest Piece of Shrapnel?). The panel of judges – Marty, Tommy and Billy – discussed each stash in hushed tones, hands behind backs, heads nodding and shaking. They carefully measured the displayed pieces with a long bit of string. I held my breath and whispered a prayer. The judges lined up. Serious faces waited behind a burnt back door stood on bricks, our makeshift table holding the awards.

In his best judge's voice, Marty boomed across the bomb site.

"And the First Prize Winner is... Punch and Johnny! Congratulations, lads!"

Our foot-long bit of shrapnel beat the lot of them! We'd won the street's competition. My gang of mates leapt on me and Punch, whooping, cheering, laughing. Someone yanked me up on Billy's shoulders and Punch was piled onto Marty's. They took us on a lap of honour round the bombsite in the late afternoon heat.

We got our prize off Marty's Grandad. A huge tin of liquorice torpedoes his Ma had somehow found. Best of all was the cardboard star hanging off a red-and-blue striped ribbon made by our Cath, and tied round our Punch's neck.

The yellow star read: "WINNER. KIRKDALE'S BEST"

Punch was the real star of the show, of course. We cracked open the tin of sweets and our gang sat munching in the shade of rubble.

Heavy footsteps pounded round the corner. "Lads, lads, where are yer?" Tony came flying on to our den, his Ma's shopping bag swinging on his shoulder. He went crashing straight into Pete's stash of shrapnel and bits and pieces of metal scattered all over the show. Tony went head over heels, landing upside-down, and his Ma's bag clonked him on the side of his head. We fell about laughing. Chewed-up liquorice dribbled down my chin. Tony picked himself up, cursing. Hopping about, rubbing his foot, he bit back a few swear words. But he clung on to his Ma's bag like his life depended on it.

"Guess what I've got lads?" He swaggered over with a smug grin.

We sprang up like a bunch of Jack in the boxes.

The pink glow of sun, low now on the horizon, cast long flickering shadows behind Tony. Strange shapes wavered off the peculiar piles of shrapnel circling him. What secrets were inside his Ma's shopping bag? Dogs howled somewhere up Lathom Steet. A pale ale bottle quietly rolled past the scattered heaps of shrapnel. A sliver of pink sunlight struck the shopping bag as Tony gently laid it down.

"What's in there, Tony?" whispered Bombo Mac.

"Shhhh," hushed Tony. "You'll find out in a minute but yer've gotta shurrup and close yer eyes." He liked a bit of drawn-out drama, did Tony.

We knelt down in a circle around the mysterious shopping bag, with its handles dropped to the sides. The pale ale bottle rolled into the circle and stopped next to the bag. We closed our eyes tight shut. The only thing that concerned us was what was in that bloody bag! Fumbling with the zip, Tony slowly opened it up. Thrusting both hands in he gently eased out its contents.

He stepped back without a word. We breathed quietly. At last, Tony said we could open our eyes. For a moment we didn't speak. We leaned forward and dared to touch it.

The bloody thing was daunting! Sitting there in the middle of our den was the biggest German Helmet in the world! It had to be! It was bloody enormous. The helmet was passed around our gang for closer inspection. We howled laughing when it didn't fit any of us."

"They must have bloody big heads those Germans!" laughed Tommy.

"And bloody square ones as well!" tittered Lenny. "Look at the bloody stupid shape of it! Definitely more square than round."

"Come on Punch, wake up lad. Try this helmet on fer size!"

The massive helmet wobbled on Punch and ended up swinging under his chin like a horse's nose- bag. I threw in some liquorice torpedoes

Tony's older brother was a Desert Rat serving in the Irish Guards. Fighting in the deserts of North Africa he unearthed the German helmet and had brought it home as a gift for Tony. That helmet gave us kids and adults hours and hours of laughs. Best of all it bought us kids a whole load of favours!

Everyone wanted to wear it. But no matter how many heads it sat on we couldn't find a head big enough to fit it. It dangled over Tony's wrist like a tin handbag and came everywhere with us.

On our way home that night we passed the sugar factory, Tate and Lyle on Love Lane, not far from the docks. Sneaking in the empty yard we went slyly searching for any loose sugar, hoping one of the large sacks had burst. All was quiet and we almost got away with a few pockets full of sugar when the booming voice of the night watchman rang out.

The big booted cocky watchman nabbed us. But spotting the German Helmet on Tony's wrist he burst out laughing. "'Ere," he laughed. "Lend us that fer a minute, lad, it'll give me mates a good laugh. God knows we need one!" Off he trotted into the factory and howls of laughter rang out.

When he returned he had filled Tony's helmet up to the top with sugar. "Get that home to yer Ma's and let them make yiz a tasty treat. Best laugh we've had in the factory for ages. Tell yer what though, son, they've got some bloody big heads them Germans!"

Ma made me and my mates toffee apples that night with the free sugar from Tate and Lyle's. As I sat in the easy chair munching away on the toffee, I wondered where Tony's Tin Hat would take us next.

* * * *

Later that same spring, on a brisk but bright afternoon, as I kicked the shattered bottles off the pavement in Lemon Street and into the gutter, not wanting Punch to cut his paws, we encountered a bunch of shawlies. A group of Irish, Catholic immigrants – hardy ladies, selling oddments from a handcart – these women were known fondly as 'shawlies' because of the thick woollen black shawls they wore. They often sold their goods along the Dock Road and Great Homer Street Market, but every now and then they wandered further into Kirkdale's terraced streets. I had been kicking along the pavement, inhaling the scent of rice pudding from someone's kitchen. Nutmeg burning nicely. "Bet that makes a lovely crispy skin," I said to Tony, and licked me lips.

At this point, one of the shawlies, an ancient stick-thin lady with wrinkles and not a tooth in her head, ran over to us, yelling out, "Give us a go of yer helmet, son."

A few of our Lemon Street friends are in this one.

The other shawlies, gathered outside the pawn shop, ran over to join her. Tony was left speechless when she yanked the German helmet off his wrist.

"We've heard all about this German helmet of yours, lad, an' I've been dyin' to get me 'ands on it. 'Ere, Mary, over 'ere gurl," she called out to another shawlie. "Go an' grab some big spoons off me 'andcart will yer, queen, an' beat me out a tune. Yer brilliant on the spoons, luv. I feel a song comin' on me!"

"I tell yer what," shouted the tallest shawlie, "I'll get me a bit of Izal toilet paper off Mrs Williams in the end house and I've got me comb in me pocket so I can give yiz a tune as well."

Some people could get a great tune out of a piece of toilet paper wrapped around a comb by blowing through it. It had to be Izal toilet paper as that was thick and shiny, like tracing paper. Ma had shown me a million times how to play it but I was hopeless, the best I could manage was a half-hearted whistle. Ma said me sucking function needed improving.

The doors in Lemon Street flew open and the growing crowd on the pavement became loud and excited.

"What yer gonna sing us for us, queen?" cried Mrs Flannigan, the stocky, white-haired lady from number twelve.

The toilet-paper-comb musician blew out a hearty whistle while the lady with the spoons beat a bass rhythm on knobbly knees. Clapping and tapping rippled through the crowd and the stick thin lady with not a tooth in her head shoved on Tony's German helmet and cut a mean Irish jig, singing loudly 'Me And My Gal'.

The skinny, toothless shawlie was a showstopper and soon had everyone on their feet, dancing, singing, howling. Lemon Street was alive with laughter. Mrs McKenna from number twenty-one trotted out with trays of tea, cakes and jam butties. A crate of pale ale was brought out of number thirty-two by Cokey the Coalman. Paddy, the one-legged man in a wheelchair from the end house dragged out his accordion. They knew how to party in Lemon Street, and any excuse would do.

It took Tony ages to retrieve his German helmet off the Irish shawlie and he only managed to do so with the promise of a return visit and another Irish jig. And we did return. Quite a few times, with me Ma, Aunty Julia and our other friends and neighbours from Flinders Street, and we always had a whale of a time. Those 'Jiggin' afternoons with the German helmet stretched into late nights, too. The helmet suffered a few battered dents from bouncing on the pavement with more than just a bottle of pale ale.

As that spring stretched into summer me and my mate, Bombo Mac, were taken with idea of having a job for our six weeks' summer holiday. It wasn't so much that I fancied the idea of work, more like the neighing of horses which drew me to Billy's Dairy.

He was a bit of an odd ball was Billy, really. He stood much more than six foot tall with a mop of ginger hair and a long wiry beard that almost reached his narrow chest. He looked like a man who spent more time in the boxing ring as a featherweight than sitting in front of the fire at home. His face had a hard, pinched look as if he saw everything in the world and approved of nothing. His calloused hands were wrinkled and suntanned, fingers long and wide like a bunch of pork sausages. He spoke little but on a good day you'd hear him chuckle at some private joke, his cheeks turning rosy if only for a brief time. And when he did laugh he revealed sparkling teeth a movie star might envy.

"Aww God love him, Johnny," said Ma, softly. "Billy's got a heart of gold underneath all that bluster, luv. Lord knows he's been given a terrible deal of the cards. Once yer get to know him luv you'll see his bright side, mark my words, son."

I was more concerned with the horses, wondering if I could ride them like John Wayne.

Billy owned a dairy and wanted a couple of helpers for his milk round. He had three black and white cows and two horses, one black and a lively bright chestnut whose thick tail brushed the floor. Best of all, Billy said we could drive his pony and trap. Now I could be a real cowboy!

Dick was the larger horse, jet black with a serious face like he had all the worries of the world. His eyes followed you closely, glossy as coal and grumpy as hell. If you didn't give him a wide berth he'd take a nibble on your leg or shoulder and think nothing of it.

On the other hand Bob, the smaller chestnut, was as calm as a cucumber and gentle as a lamb. With a few missing front teeth she smiled a beautiful grin. Dick and Bob could hear us running up to Billy's Dairy early each morning and would neigh and whinny, stomping their hooves like a marching band on parade, waiting impatiently for the handful of treats stuffed in our pockets. Carrots were their favourite but a turnip came a close second. I loved those horses and experienced all kinds of wild adventures, real and imagined for a whole, wonderful six weeks.

Billy turned out to be a great boss once we'd got to know each

Trotting along Wessie Road.

other, the best boss two young boys could ever hope for. He surprised us one morning appearing without his beard. All shaved off and bare chinned he looked like a whole different man and far less scary.

Me and Bombo Mac took turns a piece at driving the pony and trap back to the stables in Billy's Dairy. We trotted easily along the full length of Westminster Road, the wind blowing in our hair. I imagined I was John Wayne and Bombo Mac was Gabby Hayes. We imagined we were driving a stage coach under attack from the Indians. Whooping and jeering, Bob and Dick's manes flew through the air, blowing wild in hot pursuit of the hidden enemy lurking between shops and alleys and pubs at each corner. Especially the Goat's Head in Great Mersey Street, where those Indians congregated in almost invisible clusters. Dick and Bob's tails swung and swished side by side in perfect harmony. Chasing the Indians, fast and furious, hooves clattering and clopping as the race in time played out. *Yee haw!* we hollered wildly along Wessie Road. Waving my cowboy hat in circles of victory I stood up tall with the reins in one hand and plonked on my cowboy hat at a jaunty angle. It made no odds that it was an old flat cap of me Da's, to me it was the best Stetson in the whole Wild West.

Wonderful, adventurous days surrounded us lads during those six weeks of summer bliss with Billy, Dick and Bob. I could escape into a time and a land of make-believe where war no longer existed.

But in those quiet moments, just before sleep arrived, the same question was always my last thought. *When will my Da come home?*

CHAPTER 15

HOPE ON THE RAYS

July 24, 1943

Hopes of an in end in sight continued into the second half of 1943. People kept their spirits high, and escapism through our own entertainment helped alleviate anxiety in the streets of Kirkdale. We listened to music on borrowed gramophones. We danced and sang in each other's homes. We told jokes and stories, playing whatever instruments we could get our hands on. We did what we could to keep morale up whenever moods began to flag or wear thin, all of us hanging on for that great 'afterwards' that, we were promised, was almost in sight.

When the long school holidays came round, Tuesday mornings were time for just me and my Ma. We made weekly trips into Liverpool to collect her allotment money, a weekly allowance for housekeeping from my Da's employer. Brother Jimmy deemed himself far too big now for trips out with his Ma. He stayed with the other big lads, doing whatever big lads did best. Our Cath stayed at home with Aunty Julia, minding our Punch and Judy.

I loved those Tuesdays with me Ma. Just me and her, chatting away all day. Ma had me in pleats of laughter from start to finish with her funny tales and ghost stories that chilled me to the bone. We took in the sights of Liverpool's town centre and for a whole day, once a week, our minds felt free from the troubles of War. Ma made those Tuesdays special.

The number 16 tram always picked us up at the bottom of Flinders Street early in the morning, and Ma bought two tickets to the Pier Head.

The Number 16 tram to the Pier Head
was an old bone rattler.

People called this tram the old bone-shaker. When my teeth rattled all the way through town I understood why. It was ancient and hanging on by the skin of its teeth. We idled around the Pier Head watching sailing ferries bobbing up and down on the murky waters of the River Mersey.

"Nothing like a good old wind to blow the cobwebs away, eh, Johnny?" said Ma, clutching tight hold of her best silk headscarf.

"But why must it be windy *every* flamin' Tuesday, Ma?" I moaned, rubbing a speck of grit out my eye. She laughed and grabbed my hand. We strolled up and over to the Strand, or the Goree as it was locally known. I didn't know why the long road had that name, but Ma said it was where they once chained poor slaves. We stared at the rusty chains, still fixed tight into thick stone walls. We spoke of how awful the slave trade was and how shocking it was to think it wasn't that long ago.

We dawdled further into the commercial side of town. The hustle and bustle of smartly dressed office workers in full fling. The comings and goings in the busy shipping offices blurred our eyes. Bodies all in a rush, with bundles of brown envelopes shoved under their arms. Office messenger boys scuttling from building to building delivering urgent notes. Posh men and ladies in suits and high heels, bowler hats and umbrellas walked gracefully through revolving glass doors in some of the buildings. "They must have very important meetings to attend," said me Ma. The chatter of office workers buzzed through open windows; the clackety-clack from dozens of typewriters.

We stood and looked up in awe at the Liver Building.

"Let's have a quiet moment Johnny, luv," whispered Ma. "Think of all the men bravely taking care of us."

The two magical birds stood majestically on top of the Liver building, guarding sailors as they left port. "To keep them safe in raging war and troubled seas," said Ma, gripping my hand. The same mysterious birds would welcome them home too, we hoped and prayed. We left the Liver Birds, making the sign of the cross as we went.

Further up on James Street we climbed the stone steps into my Da's shipping office: Moss Hutchinson Line, Shipping Company. The highly polished brass plaque shone like a mirror set in a black, glossy oak door.

Mr Roberts, a thick set man in glasses with thinning sandy hair met us in his small office upstairs. His long wooden desk took up most of the room. Papers spilled all over the top of his desk. The room was stuffy, and smoke-filled. An ashtray over-flowing with dog-ends. One tiny window set high up by the ceiling let in just a small glint of light. I'd never seen the window open, even on roasting hot days.

Mr Roberts counted out Ma's three pounds slowly, placing them carefully into her outstretched hand. Never once could we get a smile out of Mr Roberts or anything more than a begrudging, "Good Mornin'".

"Miserable old bugger," laughed Ma when we hurried down the steps and flew back outside.

With her weekly stash tucked safely in her best handbag, Ma and I strolled up Church Street to the busy shops. Music drifted quietly from some of the open doorways, a wireless playing here and there. Crowds of shoppers milled around and chatted merrily, watching the world go by. Plenty of pigeons scrabbled about around the shoppers' feet searching for any stray crumbs. It was warmer on this side of town, out of the wind from across the Mersey.

The best part of Tuesdays was the lunchtime treat in Woolworths, the big shop where you could get anything from a mouth organ to cough drops and everything was kept under sixpence. There were still counters of stuff to browse through, despite the short supply of goods. Ma made sure she came home with a bottle of Aunt Sally's Disinfectant every fortnight.

We tucked into a lovely cup of tea for Ma in the cafeteria and a glass of yellow lemonade for me in a posh, tall glass. It had to be Schofield, though, my favourite lemonade. We often got a lovely plate of hot buttered buns. The waitress was an elegant, tall lady called Rita. A vision of loveliness, I thought, in her maroon red uniform and frilly white apron and cap. She had a bright, cheerful voice and remembered our names every week. She beamed when she brought our tray over to the table: "Enjoy yer lovely treat, Johnny, it's a joy to see yer smile. Get that nice cuppa down yer, Emily, and take the weight of yer feet, girl."

After Woollies we played a game of 'What If?' through the shop windows. What if we were rich, what luxuries would we buy? We laughed at the daft things we could indulge ourselves in if only we were rich and famous.

We dawdled over to Lime Street by the big pub on the corner. The Vines, *Where the infamous Maggie May plied her street trade luring many a drunken sailor*, said me Ma. *Robbin' the soft buggers' cash by hook or by crook.*

Ma burst into Maggie's song as we stared at The Vines Pub.[10]

"Maggie May, Maggie May," Ma hollered at the top of her voice and tapped her feet.

"They've taken her away!
She'll never walk down Lime Street anymore,
She robbed so many sailors,
And Captains of the Whalers.
Tra la la la la!"

I looked up at Ma and we both doubled up, laughing.

I wasn't exactly sure what this Maggie May lady had done and I didn't have a clue what a lady of the night was and me Ma said I was too young to know anyway. But it must've been something wicked I imagined 'cos me Ma said Maggie May ended up in prison.

The newspaper boy lingered outside Central Station, yelling, "*ECHO!* SPECIAL *ECHO!* READ ALL ABOUT IT!"

Ma thrust three half-pennies in my hand. "Pick us up an *Echo*, luv, best see what's happening eh?" I grabbed a copy and Ma scanned the headlines quickly before folding it neatly and stuffed it in her large handbag.

---

[10] 'Maggie May' is a Liverpool folk song about a prostitute who robbed a 'homeward bounder', a sailor coming home from a round trip. Maggie started her working life selling bunches of flowers and singing outside Liverpool's theatres aged just six. The older Maggie went on to be a well-known streetwalker, plying her trade outside The Vines pub by Lime Street Station. The pub's manager turned a blind eye to Lime Street's streetwalkers; they brought him great trade, not only with sailors, but with labouring men and 'slummers' (toffs dressed as working men). Some men came to the pub not only for the booze and singalongs but for the age-old pleasures of the flesh – like the sorry sailor who picked up Maggie May that fated night. With his wages in his pocket Maggie took him to her lodgings. When he awoke, hungover, the following morning, she had taken all his money and even his clothes, insisting they were in Kellys Locker, a pawn shop. When he failed to find his clothes in the pawn shop, he contacted the police. Maggie May was found guilty and sentenced to transportation to Botany Bay.

Further up the road was pretty, well-known Lizzie. She'd been flogging flowers from a handcart on the same spot for years and years. Everyone knew Lizzie, famous for her yellow roses, red carnations, pink geraniums – she had the lot. Buckets of white daisies and beautiful blooms. A perfumed smell wafted over and run up my nose.

"One day, Johnny," said me Ma, "when we're flush and have a spare bob or two I'd love to treat us to a bunch of those lovely flowers. Mind you luv, I'd better get a vase first, eh?"

We laughed, but I silently promised myself that one day, I would treat me Ma to the best bunch of flowers in the world.

The famous Adelphi Hotel stood before us in all its splendour. "Kings and Queens have stayed here, yer know, Johnny. They could've even walked in this very spot were stood on. Can yer imagine that, luv?" Ma bowed as if we were Kings and Queens ourselves.

We ended up at the tram stop and waited for our ride back out of town. Ma wrapped her arms around my shoulder and smiled. "It's been a great day again, hasn't it, Johnny? But I bet yer our Punch is goin' to go mad when he sees yer."

"I know, Ma," I said, "He'll be doin' his nut! He'll wash our faces off when he clocks us!"

Ma opened her big handbag. "Better get me hanky ready to wipe off all his slobber."

The tram came rumbling along and took us home for another week.

* * * *

The summer holidays slipped away all too quickly. It was time to return to Daisy Street School, move up a class, and meet our new teacher.

Miss Hannah put the fear of God into us kids. The thought of her teaching us was terrifying. She hovered around in the playground on that first day back to school. Silent and quick, steel-grey beady eyes taking each of us in. She could freeze you out with just one look from those ice-cold eyes. Her gun-metal hair matched those eyes perfectly.

I was sick to the stomach waiting in the playground and was terrified my morning's porridge would return in front of all my mates. I feared her as much as I feared the dentist in Great Mersey Street, Dr Baker, the butcher dentist who pulled your teeth out without giving you enough gas.

How in God's name will I survive a *whole* school year with this awful battle-axe? I wanted to turn around and flee back home to the safety of our Punch.

Splodges of rain dribbled down the back of my neck and I forced my legs to move forward to the shelter of the doorway I didn't want to walk through. I turned to glance at Bombo Mac running towards me. His eyes were wide and white, darkened shadows beneath his cheeks made them appear hollow and sunken. He gave me a nervous smile.

"Are yer ready to tackle the big Miss Freeze, Johnny? Let's get it over and done with, eh? Let's walk in together. We'll pretend were John Wayne and Gabby Hayes again. We can do that, can't we, Johnny?"

I thrust my hands deep in my pockets and closed one eye. "Sure can, Gabby, let's go ride 'em, cowboy!"

We swallowed the huge lumps in our throats and like two brave cowboys put our best booted feet forward and swaggered ahead just as the bell rang loud and clear.

Ma had urged me earlier not to worry about my new teacher and to put my fears aside.

"First impressions can be misleading," she said. "Never judge a book by its cover, son, or you'll never get to know what's really inside. Give the lady a chance and look for the good in her. Be kind, polite and friendly. She'll be eatin' out of yer hands in no time at all, mark my words, son. Most of all, Johnny, always be yer lovely self."

Ma was right, of course. Mrs Hannah's freezing front really was just a mask to cover her shyness and once she thawed out she could even be warm as toast. Well, sometimes.

Best of all, we discovered the shy Miss Hannah had a secret…

Who let the cat out of the bag?

Drifting and dreaming in a late afternoon class, the sun was making me sleepy. I squinted with one eye half-shut, shifting in my seat to stay awake. I yawned, stretched my legs out, and shook my head to blow away the cobwebs. I noticed Miss Hannah's handbag wide open beneath her desk; some of its contents had spilled out. I recognized two packets of cigarettes in red-and-white cartons. A camel laughing: American issue Camel cigarettes. They lay there with a red lipstick tube and a round, gold make-up mirror like the one me Ma used on special days, the one with pinkish powder and a sponge inside.

A little grin crept on to my face. I never expected to see that in a month of Sundays, not from *her*! It looked like our posh, shy, Miss Hannah was hanging around with the handsome Yanks! She must have been to get hold of those packets of Camel ciggies. Well, I couldn't wait to tell my mates at playtime. *I bet yer she's with the Officers though*, I thought. And I couldn't for the life of me imagine Miss Hannah puffing away on a ciggy. I bet she used one of those long swanky cigarette holders like the glamorous ladies in the movies.

Something else suddenly dawned on me. I bet Miss Hannah has gone and fallen head over heels in love with an officer. *That's* why she's suddenly got all warmed up. It made sense now. My mates agreed in our hush-hush after-school meeting in our den. If we knew who the new officer boyfriend was we could thank him. He'd definitely been a gentleman for buttering up the once-frosty Miss Freeze. None of us were ever scared of her again and like butter in our hands she melted.

* * * *

"Don't yer be goin' anywhere near that den of iniquity, Johnny luv. D'yer hear me now?"

"Course not, Ma." As if!

The year was passing and we were seeking new entertainment this autumnal afternoon. The Brisbane Club was infamous. A place where anything goes. Despite Ma's warnings the pull of this drinking club on the corner of Stanley Road drew us kids like a magnet, though none of us knew what a den of iniquity was.

Soldiers, sailors and airmen burst through its heavy doors on the lookout for a good time. Desperate for a night to remember, a welcome relief. Some pretty wild times went on inside that smoky place with windows you couldn't see through. Wild times that spilled out and on to the streets. We kids hovered outside in shadowed corners, watching the antics open-mouthed from a safe distance. The drunken brawls were fiercer than any saloon fight I'd watched in Western movies. Men and women fought tooth and nail in a haze of whiskey and gin. Cat-fights and handbags at dawn.

But we kids loved the action and drama of those drunken nights outside the club. To us, it was like watching a real life Wild West movie. The Brisbane Club had many raids from the military police. British, French, Polish and American: the military was always on the lookout for deserters. Sadly, we saw many young lads – boys, really – dragged off to God knows where.

The American Military Police were typical Yanks in our young eyes. Over the top and seven feet tall. Armed of course and they meant business. They drove up to the Brisbane Club in armoured jeeps and burst through its doors, dragging out a load of unsuspecting G.I.s and beating them ruthlessly with wooden batons. It was horrific and unmerciful: a terrible sight to witness.

Even long after the War had ended Ma still called the Brisbane Club a den of iniquity, its reputation hard to shake off. Though it did stay open, it became much quieter over the following years.

As I grew up I thought about The Brisbane Club and reflected on those memories through adult eyes. Those men were just ordinary guys having a good time in dreadful circumstances, grabbing a bit of fun while they could. None of them knew what tomorrow would bring. They could be shipped overseas without warning and could be blown to pieces in the blink of an eye. They lived for the moment; it was all they really had. Looking back, it is clear that those Yanks saved our bacon many times, and we will always be grateful. God Bless them all.

* * * *

As the year drew to a close, we had a rare letter from my Uncle Jimmy, Ma's older brother. Like my Da, Jimmy was a seafarer. At only fourteen years of age Uncle Jimmy knew that life on the seas was his natural calling. He was partial to a drop of beer and whiskey.

"Bedfellows!" Ma said, twisting her lip. "That's what the bottle and our Jimmy are." But he was a kind, generous man with a heart of gold; an eccentric character who would have you in fits of laughter. I can honestly say I never once saw him sober, yet he was always fully in control.

"He was born with the luck of the Irish, he was," Ma smiled. It was true. Uncle Jimmy escaped many a hairy situation. All he ever wanted was to be at sea with his booze. He lived for it. Ma said he was oblivious that we were even at war.

He sailed in all the dangerous convoys in the Atlantic Ocean. It was a miracle he survived the four times his ship was torpedoed. He spent four days adrift in freezing waters without a life-jacket, but with a keg of whiskey strapped round his neck. He said the whiskey kept him afloat when he was finally rescued, completely unfazed! He did end up hating swimming though.

Uncle Jimmy became something of a lucky mascot to his superstitious sea-faring mates. "We might get hit," they said, "but if Jimmy's aboard we'll do alright!"

"Our Jimmy will never swallow the anchor, luv, he's too bloody well-preserved in whiskey!" Ma hooted.

Me Ma was right and Uncle Jimmy survived the War to tell another tale and remained at sea for the rest of his days - with a bottle of whiskey to keep him warm!

CHAPTER 16

AS TIME GOES BY

15 January, 1944

We dithered at the window, freezing to the bone, Ma's arms stretched around us, held tight in a shivering huddle; squashed together for warmth and protection. Punch trembled across our feet. Wild black clouds rolled across the almost-purple sky, fast and furious, raging blindly from the deepest reaches of the River Mersey. Screaming in pain when forked lightning stabbed right through the heart of the peculiar clouds. Prongs of flickering, silver anger pierced their very centre and they groaned miserably in darkened grief.

Ma quickly drew the curtains and bustled us under the table. Hailstones hammered ruthlessly, drumming a heavy beat on the roof. Drops of slimy grey water seeped through the kitchen ceiling. A fresh clap of thunder pushed us further beneath the table, and I gripped Punch's neck. Cath cried out. Punch moved over to Cath, curling up on her knees to protect her and licking away her frightened tears.

We were terrified on that terrible, dark and stormy night. The third clap of thunder sent Ma's picture of pretty flowers above the fireplace smashing to the floor. Ma leapt out from under the table, clearing up the shards of glass. Snatching a red blanket from the easy chair she retreated back under the table as quick as she could.

A burnt smell hovered through the room and swept under the table, thick and cloying. Ma said it was electricity from the forked lightening. The yellow glow from the gas mantle cast shadows, long and flickering, across our floor and up the darkened walls.

"Dancing Devils," whispered Jimmy, and Cath screamed once more. Punch barked at Jimmy and Ma swung a clip around his ear. Only one thing was certain. There wasn't a cat in hell's chance of any of us coming out from under our table.

Ma kept us tightly bound in the old red blanket which smelled more of Punch than us.

With the next clap of thunder came an unmerciful pounding on our front door.

"Let me in! Let me in! Emily, let me in, girl!"

"*Jesus, Mary and Joseph*!" Ma cried out, untangling herself from the blanket. "Who in God's name is out on a night like this?"

"Let me in! Let me in!" The screeches rose louder with the hammering knocks.

The hairs stood up on Punch's back and he took on the stance of a fierce protector, lips stretched in a low, guttural growl.

"Watch the kids, Punch," Ma shouted. "Keep them safe, lad!" Ma trembled as she flew out to see who on Earth was rapping on our door.

"For the love of Mary!" she roared out, as somebody fell through the door.

"What the hell are yer doin' out at this time of night? Get yerself inside now. Granny Murphy, 'ave yer gone daft in the head or somethin'?"

Granny Murphy was pushed ungraciously into the room, and Ma dragged off her soaking wet coat.

"I missed me bleedin' tram, didn't I, Emily!"

Ma furiously rubbed Granny Murphy's head with a big old towel.

"Where the flamin' hell 'ave yer been, luv? Get them clothes off now while I get yer a warm dress and cardy. 'Ere Jimmy, get the pan on to boil, quick, lad. Make us all a nice, hot cup of tea."

Ma quickly got Granny Murphy into warm, dry clothes and shoved her own fluffy slippers onto Granny's big feet.

"I was at the Church meeting at St Ollie's, wasn't I, girl? I was that busy gabbin' to Mrs Kennedy in the porch when the last tram flew past quicker than I could run. Then the bloody heavens opened. Like a drowned bloody rat I was, stuck halfway between here and there. It was too far fer me to get all the way home in one piece, Emily. I saw yer light glowing, God bless yer for bein' home, luv."

Ma snatched the red blanket from under the table and wrapped it around Granny Murphy's shoulders. "Get that round yer before yer get bloody pneumonia."

Jimmy came struggling in with a cup of hot tea in each hand.

"Well yer'll not be goin' home tonight, gerl. Yer can share a nice warm bed with our Cath and get yer 'ead down 'ere".

"Ah, yer a good one Emily, luv, yer've got a heart of gold." Granny Murphy poured the hot tea in to the only saucer we had. Blowing loudly, she took a big slurp.

At least the thunder and lightning had stopped. The rain still beat down, but we felt safe enough to come out from under the table and join Ma and Granny Murphy around the easy chair.

Big drops of rain plopped like a dripping tap into the metal mop bucket Ma had shoved beneath the leaking ceiling.

By the time Granny Murphy had slurped her tea, the rain had softened to almost a light shower. The skies had quietened. We huddled around each other in the soft yellow glow of our room. Punch settled and was now snoring. The room had warmed with the extra body heat and Cath yawned loudly.

"Why don't yer get yerself off to bed, Cath, luv? Come on, little lady, Punch can sleep with you till Granny Murphy's ready for some shut eye. He'll keep yer all snug and warm, luv."

Punch bolted up and over to Cath, wagging his tail. Cath was made up, she didn't often get the chance to have Punch share her bed. He always slept with me.

Ma tucked them in and by the time she said *Goodnight and God Bless*, the pair of them were snoring for England.

Ma sat on the floor with me and Jimmy next to Granny Murphy in the easy chair and wriggled her toes in me Da's slippers.

Granny Murphy must be at least a hundred, I thought, judging by the dozens of wrinkles lining her thin face. She sucked noisily on her teeth and I noticed how much like her son she was. She had the same long arms as Monk Murphy. The same huge feet. The same wide grin with big yellow teeth. Granted, Granny Murphy didn't have quite as many teeth as Monk, but nevertheless they were exactly the same. She was as tall as Monk, with her frizzy hair tied up in a tangled bun like a doughnut. She stroked a gnarled set of reddish-blue knuckles over Ma's warm blanket.

She and Monk shared the same kind heart, and the same love of story-telling. Granny Murphy was famous her for ghost stories. *The ones that make you shiver*, Ma said, rather fond of telling ghost stories herself; Aunty Julia, too. Mrs Murphy's Irish lilt brought a soft musical tone to her ghostly tales.

"Well, wouldn't yer be thinkin', Emily, that it's the perfect night to be hearin' all about the Irish Wailin' Banshees now?"

Granny Murphy's sea blue eyes twinkled and danced.

"I'd say it's the perfect night for sure. What about you, kids? Fancy a spooky tale off Granny Murphy, eh?" Oh, yes we did! We snuggled around the easy chair and sat in mesmerized silence.

"*On the stormy Irish seas…*" Granny Murphy whispered while the flames flickered and cackled in the hearth. "When dark and violent nights brought howling winds. Gales whipped sailing boats to death and destruction…

"Those were the darkened nights the sailors feared most. And no amount of prayers would save them. They knew this.

"At first, they thought it was nothing more than a deeper moaning and groaning of the caustic winter air that swept itself through their ears. But it began to change, like a terrible haunting lullaby. The wails ebbed and flowed like the crashing waves that spilled over their moonlit ship. The wails hid muffled, strangled words and the sailors froze, straining to listen against the ceaseless wind and unforgiving, ruthless storm. Forks of fiery lightening burnt upon the surface of tormented seas. But still the Banshees spoke in haunted wails, watching, waiting, eager to claim their latest sailors. They spoke with no language the sailors knew of, but they knew only too well that the torturous wails could only ever bring no good deed. For it was the souls of the sailors they craved for their own terrible survival.

"From the stormy blackness of the skies came the wails that no living thing could ever make. They perhaps were once alive, in some kind of a hell, but now rendered into some obscene spirits that contorted and wreathed in eternal pain, anger and hatred. As the silvery wisps of the Wailing Banshees curled in around the ship, the wails grew stronger, much closer now. The sailors huddled together, eyes squeezed tight shut in terror, hands clamped over their ears, but still hearing everything none the less. Petrified in the face of certain death, the sailors screamed uselessly, screams drowning beneath the noise of the Banshees' Wails

The sailors knew the Wails of The Banshees wouldn't cease until every last dying breath was sucked away, stolen for another kind of hell. The last crash of the storm suddenly stilled the seas and the lightening was gone, as were the terrible wails, leaving only no movement of the sailors in the frozen ship; only broken bodies, washed up on the silent shores beneath the pale moonlight."

Granny Murphy slurped the last dregs of her tea in the saucer. "Time for bed, luvs?"

* * * *

Sweat dripped off my nose and splashed onto the cracked, grey pavements like a big blob of snot. My bloody feet were wrecked but it made no odds. Ma said I just had to *get on with it and stop moanin'.* The long, hard slog across the back streets of Liverpool must be made. My shoulders and back screamed in pain and my arms hung off me, aching and sore. It's that bloody glass box's fault. Sitting there like a big, fat elephant on top of me Ma's cabinet, our name written on its top in screaming red paint. I hated this job. That accumulator laughed at me like a one-eyed monster every time its juice ran out. Cackled it did, like that old witch haunting the graveyard in Rodney Street. Ma's yells came every week and I'd have to take the accumulator all the way up to the radio shop to be topped up. It weighed a bloody ton! But life wasn't worth living in our house if the wireless wasn't working.

As most homes didn't have a television set during the War, the wireless – radio – was the main form of communication and entertainment. Eight out of ten people owned a wireless. Besides news and information, there were music programmes, talks and comedy shows. *It's That Man Again* was one of my Ma's favourites, as was *The Man In Black*, stories on a dark night that scared us witless! The famous singer Vera Lynn had her own programme. The wireless was a very important means of keeping cheerful during the terrors of the War. We didn't have any electric in our house so our wireless was the kind that ran off a battery called the accumulator. One of my weekly errands as a small boy was to take the accumulator to Bennet's Radios to get it charged up.

The accumulator was rather like a large, heavy square bottle with a handle on the top. Inside were the components that made it work, surrounded by acid. Our old-fashioned wireless had a long wire that stretched across the room and outside the house – the aerial which picked up a radio signal.

Earlier that afternoon, Ma had interrupted me just as I was rolling my best ollie towards a winning shot. "Johnny! *Johnny!*" she screeched across the street.

"Blast!" I cursed to Punch who looked up, his eyes shining in sympathy. He knew what was coming. I hauled myself up from the kerb and miserably pocketed my best ollie. Punch dragged his heels.

"Johnny! Hurry up, lad," Ma summoned atop the door-step. "Get up to Bennet's Radios!"

I groaned and braced myself. Flexed my arms and dragged myself indoors. Cath hummed quietly in the corner making a rag rug from Da's old shirts. "*Swinging On A Star,*" she sang sweetly. I wished *I* was swingin' on a bloody star.

I grabbed the accumulator off the china cabinet and reminded myself and not to spill the battery acid down my jumper. I did that to my best blue jumper last month. When Ma washed it, it fell to bits and she blew her top.

"Be bloody careful, Johnny! That acid will burn yer skin off and yer'll end up lookin' like a slice of fried bacon an' end up in Stanley Ozzy!"

Apple pie was baking on the fire, reminding me of the hot toffee Kim Singh sold in long, stringy strands on a Saturday afternoon in Great Homer Street's busy market. He wore a white cotton shirt down to his ankles, with matching trousers. A white turban covered his wide head and it had a gold, oval jewel in the middle. The peculiar jewel sparkled like a star and he said it came from a sacred, ancient cave in India. It also gave him magical powers, he smiled. His home-made bike contraption doubled as a mobile oven with a metal box underneath its handles. *I'll get meself some of his toffee next week*, I thought, if I can pick up an odd job or two. The idea of hot toffee spurred me on as I lugged the accumulator awkwardly out of our house.

"Awww, thanks Johnny, luv." Ma leaned on the kitchen door up to her elbows in flour and shouted to my back. "Can't be missing '*In Town Tonight*' can we, eh?" Ma would have our guts for garters if she missed her best weekend programme. "Aww, yer the best son a Ma could wish for Johnny, luv"

I snarled. "Don't know why our Jimmy can't do it, it's always bloody me!" I whinged under my breath – but only Punch heard me

"Come 'ead Punch, better get on with it."

Halfway down Flinders Street I plonked the accumulator by Mrs Moran's door step and leaned on her newly painted battleship-grey windowsill. It was still tacky and I yanked my elbow off quick. I only left a small smudge but thought I'd better scarper in case she'd clocked me. Mrs Ellis opposite was cleaning her windows with white stuff and scrunched-up newspaper. She was picking off wide, brown gummed paper strips, criss-crossed over the window to black it out. She'd obviously now managed to buy some black curtains to hang up. Her baby girl was helping, drawing pretty circles and smiley faces but Mrs Ellis didn't look best pleased. Punch looked up and frowned, waiting to move on.

"If only me Ma had electricity," I whispered to Punch, "We'd never have to lug this bloody thing ever again. Imagine having electricity, eh, Punch? Just plugging a radio into a switch? Sounds like magic, doesn't it, lad?" Punch wagged his tail. "An' imagine flicking a switch and lights came on in every room. Bet it'd look like permanent daylight!" Punch was sniffing something in the gutter.

Struggling across the busy Stanley Road a speeding tram flew past and we only just managed to jump out of its way in time. The wrinkly faced driver waved his hands and hat at me.

"He was goin' way too flamin' fast ,wasn't he Punch? Bloody lunatic! Must be time for his tea break."

Stacks of beer-stained crates, broken bottles, ciggy ends and smelly puddles lurked outside the Brisbane Club. We skirted around the mess and stopped outside the bike shop.

Shiny blue bikes, spokes full of racing cards, blinking bike lights.

"God, what I'd give to have a bike, Punch." He stood up on his paws, leaning on the window with his tongue hanging out.

"I'd get one with a basket on, then yer could sit in it like yer was the King of the Street. What d'yer think of that, eh?" He woofed.

"One day Punch; one day, lad."

We piled into Bennet's Radios, sweating cobs. "Thank God," I mumbled, plonking the accumulator on the counter.

Bennet's Radios was on Stanley Road.

Mr Bennet shoved back his straggly waves of long black hair and topped up the accumulator.

"That's you done fer another week, Johnny. Tell yer Ma I said hello and I'll see her in St Ollie's for Sunday Mass. I've got a bit of something' for yer Ma and Aunty Julia." He winked and held open the door and the bell tinkled.

"Ta-ra, Mr Bennet, see yer next week".

He sneaked Punch a bit of what looked like bacon fat from his overall pocket.

We stood outside the barber shop and I remembered me Ma had given me sixpence for a short back and sides. *I better get it done on Monday,* I thought, *or else she'll get the puddin' basin out and I'll look a holy show.*

I clocked little Sadie further up the street pushing that old pram of hers. She only had one shoe on.

"Sadie! Sadie, 'ere a minute, gerl!"

Sadie twisted around and backtracked over to us. Her wobbly pram refused to go in a straight line.

"Wharra yer want, Johnny?" Sadie fiddled with her doll's blanket

Our local chemist for lotions and potions.

then leaned down to Punch. Dirty skinny arms wrapped around his neck.

"Do us a favour will yer, Sadie? Put this bloody accumulator in yer pram for us. Me arms are killin' me."

"D'yer think I'm crackers or somethin' Johnny!" she squealed, horrified. "I'm not puttin' that ugly thing in me best pram, not with my Sally! She's havin' a nap!"

"Awww, come on Sadie, please. Anyway, Sadie, don't yer think it's about time yer doll woke up? Yer won't get her to sleep tonight if yer let her nap too long," I played along with her cissy girl game. "Awww, come on Sadie," I pleaded. " I'll get our Cath to teach yer how to tap-dance."

Sadie thought about it. "Well, I suppose Sally *should* be woken up, but yer better tell yer Cath to come to ours tomorrer with her tap shoes, I'll have to borrow them."

Cath and her treasured tap shoes.

Our deal was struck on the busy Stanley Road as the smell of stale beer and fish clung to our hair.

"But yer can bloody well push it yerself, Johnny. 'Ere, let me get my Sally out first."

God, I hoped none of me mates saw me pushing a bloody doll's pram. "Let's be quick, Punch, just in case. Keep dixie for me, lad. I'd never hear the end of it if me mates found out, especially if Bombo Mac clocked me…"

We raced all the way home, Sadie moaning like mad. Punch barged through our house first and I rescued the accumulator from Sadie's battered pram. She carefully tucked her Sally back under a grubby blanket that'd seen better days. I couldn't make head nor tail of what colour it once was.

"Yer've gone an got me blanket all dirty now Johnny, with that stupid box thing." She had the cheek to whinge. "I'm not letting yer lend it ever again, so there. Put that in yer pipe an' smoke it."

"Don't yer go tellin' me mates I pushed yer pram Sadie, I'm warnir yer gerl!"

"It'll cost yer, Johnny..." Sadie threw back her head and laughe all the way up our street.

"*Bloody girls!*" I mumbled to Punch. " More bleedin' trouble that they're worth!"

I plonked the charged-up accumulator back in its place, on to of me Ma's china cabinet, then slumped in our saggy easy chair an kicked off my shoes. Job done for another week. I closed my droop eyes, drifting and dreaming of a hot tin bath.

Bath Night was bliss in a tin.

CHAPTER 17

THE BEGINNING OF THE END

6 June, 1944 (D-Day)

A bright warm sun glistened off the freshly white-washed walls in our small backyard. In the right-hand corner an ancient black mangle stood out like a sore thumb.

"Oh flamin' hell, Punch, its bloody washin' day again." He whimpered at my feet. " Why cant our Jimmy help me Ma? It's always *me* who gets the rotten jobs. Not fair is it lad…"

The Allied Invasion had begun in Normandy the previous evening, on 5 June, 1944. Two groups of Allied bombers dropped tin-foil strips over Pas-de-Calais. The objective? Confuse the hell out of the German radar systems. Just after midnight, over one-and-a-half thousand tonnes of bombs were dropped on German troops in Normandy. Six-and-a-half thousand vessels sailed across the Channel with one-hundred-and-ninety-four thousand troops on board. Five beaches were given codenames – 'Sword' and 'Gold' for the British troops; 'Juno' for the Canadian troops; 'Omaha' and 'Utah' for the U.S. troops. At the end of that first day, one-hundred-and-fifty-thousand men were ready, able and waiting upon the shores. Six more weeks would see uncompromising fighting, culminating with our troops advancing out of Normandy. The foothold into occupied Europe had been established. The brilliant planning of military strategies proved victorious.

But as a young kid in the streets of Liverpool, what exactly did D-Day mean to me? At that moment in time my only focus was on luggin' that massive bucket off the fire with me Ma and into the backyard; it was hard work.

"Be careful!" she'd yell. "Don't go droppin' me bucket, Johnny, the waters pipin' hot." Well I could see that for myself!

Dozens of soapy fingers slithered over the sides but Ma kept pouring on even more scoops of Oxidol Soap powder from its blue-and-yellow box. I didn't like its smell, not one little bit. It made me sneeze all day. But we'd have to drag the bucket into the backyard and pour the steaming water into an old tin bath. Ma and Aunty Julia would scrub their hearts out all afternoon, on their knees like a pair of bookends. Sharing a ridged glass washboard between them, they'd tell jokes and stories, laughing among the soap suds

When they finished all the washin' I helped Ma empty the tin bath down the grid – and then came the bit I couldn't stand.

"Come an' give us a hand with the mangle, Johnny…"

I moaned every week but Ma *still* made me put the soppin' wet clothes through the mangle. "Watch yer fingers, soft lad," she warned. "Can't 'ave yer fingers all mashed-up in the rollers. I'm too busy to be takin' yer up to Stanley Ozzy again, luv."

I'd feed the wet clothes through one end of the mangle and Ma would catch them, less wet, at the other end, ready to peg out on the washing line. "Make sure every drop of water is wrung out, Johnny." My arms ached all night after the weekly washing day.

I knelt down next to Punch and tickled his belly.

"We've got about an hour to go before Ma wants me to bring out the bucket, Punch. Come 'ead lad, lets escape in here and read me comics fer a bit. Ma will shout us when she's ready."

I'd been up to Mrs Hendry's newsagents on Stanley Road for my comics that morning and couldn't wait to get me teeth into the *Beano*, *Hotspur*, and *Dandy*. The only place me and Punch could get any privacy was our outdoor toilet. It smelt of Aunt Sally's disinfectant and you couldn't swing a cat in it but it'd do, it was quiet.

I nudged open the toilet door with my knee and got comfy on one side of the wooden bench, the toilet bowl stuck in the middle. I noticed we were running short of toilet paper. "Must remind me Ma to cut up some newspaper squares," I mumbled to Punch

It was nice to grab a bit of silence for a bit. The streets were noisy today with crowds of people all over the show, gossiping in little clusters on street corners. It had been quite a challenge picking up my comics this morning in Stanley Road. People were shouting *"it's D-Day!"* and everyone was happy and laughing.

I tried to work out exactly what D-Day meant. I had heard Mrs Moran talking to Father John when I was picking up my comics. She was saying that we had invaded France, hoping to push back the Germans. She said a lot of brave men had died, struggling to get ashore on the beaches of Normandy. I didn't know where Normandy was. But everyone was saying that the War would soon be over, and that hope was a wonderful thing.

"We will never give up!" shouted people along Stanley Road. I sat there in our toilet hideaway stroking Punch, thinking of me Da, praying D-Day really meant the War was nearly over.

"Johnny! Johnny! Me bucket's ready, son!" Ma's cries echoed from the kitchen window.

"Bloody hell, Punch." I swiped up my pile of comics.

"Nothin' stops for me Ma's washin'. Not even bloody D-Day!"

* * * *

Sixty British soldiers, commanded by Major Roy Farran, fought their way east from Rennes towards Orleans, through German-occupied forest, forcing the Germans to retreat and aiding the French Resistance in its struggle for liberation. Code-named Operation Wallace, this push east was just another nail in the coffin of German supremacy in France. The Germans had already lost their position in Normandy, and had retreated from Southern France. Most of the German troops in the west were trapped, and were either being killed or taken prisoner in what was called the 'Falaise Pocket', a site around the Eastern town of Falaise, encircled by the Allies. The Allies were also landing tens of thousands of men and vehicles in France, and the French resistance was becoming more brazen every day. The French police force announced its loyalty to the Resistance by seizing the Prefecture de Police in Paris, raising the French national flag, and singing the 'Marseillaise', the French national anthem. Major Farran, a veteran of the fighting in Italy, employed his British Special Air Service force to burst boldly eastward from Rennes to the region just north of Orleans through the German lines of defence in order to attack the enemy from within its own strongholds. Along the way, French Resistance fighters joined the battle with him. Farren was taken aback by the strength of the French freedom fighters, and the anticipation of liberation in the air. Describing one French woman, Farran said, "Her smile ridiculed the bullets".

Heights by great men reached and kept were not obtained by sudden flight but, while their companion slept, they were toiling upward in the night.
– LONGFELLOW

* * * *

Uncle Matty's long struggle for work had come to an end in 1941 when the construction of munition factories provided employment for thousands. Uncle Matty worked a three-shift system filling shells at the Royal Ordinance Factory in Kirkby. At that time Kirkby was a rural area on the outskirts of Liverpool. Aunty Julia, with five children, was now able to remain at home, taking care of the house and children.

Throughout all the Liverpool bombings, the Christmas Blitz and the May Blitz, Uncle Matty point-blank refused to ever use an air-raid shelter. He would make sure Aunty Julia and their children were safe and secure in Ma's shelter and then go back home.

"If I'm going to die, then I'll die in my own bed," he said. He slept safe and sound through every appalling bomb raid.

But on that awful September day in 1944, so close to the end of the War, tragedy struck the munition factory in Kirkby, Liverpool, for the second time. The terrible explosion claimed the lives of fourteen men and women, including Uncle Matty and left many with horrific injuries. It took three months of work to clear four thousand bombs, buried in the rubble. A total of thirty-seven awards for bravery and distinguished conduct were awarded by the King to those who worked at the scene of the devastation.

The news of Uncle Matty's death devastated Aunty Julia and the family. Their eldest and only daughter, Annie, was pregnant at the time with her first child. The shock of losing her dear Dad in such a tragic way caused a miscarriage and she lost her longed-for baby. Annie never did have another child.

Aunty Julia sobbed in my Ma's arms in our tiny back kitchen. Me and our Jimmy rushed around, boiling pans of water, pulling out chipped cups and saucers and our brown tea-pot, making tea that nobody wanted to drink. But we needed the time, the distraction especially Aunty Julia before she could speak again. Her shaking hand clutched a rolled-up ciggy, the stinging smoke merging with the tears in her eyes. With so many people, shocked family, friends and neighbours piled in our kitchen, the shrinking size of the room reflected a good heart broken. It was a terrible irony of war was that Uncle Matty had slept safely, unharmed, while under constant enemy attack only to meet his tragic death at the hands of our own weaponry.

* * * *

Ma's old piano was dragged unceremoniously to the bottom of Flinders street by Frankie the bin-man from Bootle and Nobby McNulty the number 16 tram conductor who was already three sheets to the wind on whiskey. They pushed and shoved Ma's pride and joy without a care in the world. Ma and me Aunty Julia hovered nervously behind the staggering men; Mrs Murphy was like a cat on a hot tin roof desperate for a turn on the piano.

Finally, though, the news we had longed for had arrived – Germany had surrendered, signalling the end of World War Two. Hitler had committed suicide a week earlier, so it was left to Grand Admiral Donitz, the boss of the Third Reich for just a week, to admit defeat. He acceded unconditionally to the Allies' demands in front of senior officers from Britain, America, Russia and France. After years of misery, rationing, fear, death and horrific casualties, war-weary Britain started the party early, ahead of the official celebrations on 8 May 1945.

On our street, the neighbours rushed in and out of houses, carrying armfuls of plates, corned beef and meat paste butties, pork pies, jars of pickled onions, beetroot and bottles of brown sauce. They were piled high on a few pasting tables decked out with colourful tablecloths for a street party that would last for days. Crates of beer were tucked safely beneath tables; Monk Murphy rolled out another barrel.

When it got dark, Ma and a gang of our neighbours took us along Scotland Road to see the lights being switched on. We were all there, me and me mates, their mums and aunties – and Punch, of course. We joined the crowds of other people in a long line, doing the conga

Party, party party.

Ma and Aunty Julia celebrating with family.

through Lime Street and past the train station. The ships' horns were blowing like mad on the Mersey. Streaming past St George's Hall we saw Joe Loss and his band playing 'In The Mood'. Cath was delighted and only wished she had brought her tap shoes. We congaed all the way back to our street and saw a bonfire in Sylvester Street on our way. Loads of streets were blazing, all lit up in celebration.

We arrived back home for our own street party, more than ready to tuck in to the tasty food, and beer for the grown-ups.

"Time to let down our hair," yelled Paddy from the top of our street.

"We've bloody well waited long enough!" Mrs Kelly shouted over to Mrs Boyle who was doin' a jig with Jimmy the docker and Lilly Longshanks' pet monkey, Blinkey.

Celebrations went on all night long. Paddy fell fast asleep in his wheelchair after too much rum. Mrs McGuire fell off a doorstep trying to do a tango for one (she wasn't used to port and lemon). Ma lost her voice, Aunty Julia lost her teeth, Blinkey the monkey took too much of a shine to Mrs Moore and Jimmy the Docker passed out in next door's toilet. Punch was knackered, trying to catch next door's moggy. But no-one cared. We were happy and we laughed our heads off for days. Hitler ruled no more.

CHAPTER 18

BLOWING IN THE WIND

28 March, 1945

Ma stood at the front room window craning her neck. Tapping her foot and drumming her long fingers on the window-sill she sighed once more, the furrowed lines of her forehead creasing deeper with every huff and puff .

"Here he is! Here he is!"

She darted out of the front room and bounded over us three kids sprawled on the floor with Punch and an old sock. We leapt up and followed her to the front door. We'd been waiting every day for the last week.

Ma threw her arms around the telegram man and knocked off his hat. His pale face reddened and he gave an embarrassed chuckle. Ma tore open the envelope as we dashed back, dancing through the hall.

"Yer Da's comin' home next week!"

It was the longest week of my life. We'd already waited far too long for my Da to come home. We counted off the final seven days until at long last it finally arrived.

Ma buttered hot toast for our breakfast and Cath asked to lick the knife.

"Not on yer nelly, young lady! Where's yer manners gone?"

"Awww, Ma..." Cath simpered.

"How much longer, Ma?"

"Another hour Johnny, that's all, luv. Yer better go an' get ready, luv. Tell our Jimmy to hurry up as well. I've gotta get meself ready an' all. I've laid out me best costume already."

"Yis, Ma."

I dashed up the dancers and yelled to Jimmy who was engrossed in a book to get a move on. I pulled out my best blue jumper from the battered chest of drawers. Jimmy had already polished my boots. I quickly smoothed down my sticky-up hair and checked my face was clean in Ma's dressing table mirror.

"I'll give you a quick brush an' all, Punch. Make yer neat and tidy for me Da, eh?"

He woofed, and rolled over on Ma's bed.

"*Da's coming home, Punch! Da's coming home!*" I sang my bloody head off.

Cath looked like an Angel, me Ma said. And she did! She wore a pretty little dress with tiny orange and white flowers and a lacy collar. Ma had made it from an old dress of her own which no longer fitted. She had a long-sleeved, white cardigan on which Ma had knitted this week from wool off Aunty Julia. She'd sewn on shiny little buttons like pearls; they matched the two silk ribbons in her ringlets. Cath wanted to wear her tap shoes but Ma said no.

"The clickin' noise will drive people daft. Besides, the walk won't do the soles any good."

Jimmy swaggered down the stairs. He looked very smart but then again he always looked smart, not a bit like me. He even wore a blue tie and a white shirt of me Da's. It was a bit big in the collar but it didn't matter.

Even Punch had a new collar to meet me Da. Ma found an old brown leather belt and tied the ends together with string.

"Is it time to go yet, Ma? Are we goin' now?"

"Comin' now, Johnny."

Ma stepped slowly down the stairs in black, shiny high heels.

"Wow! Is that really you, Ma?" Jimmy smiled and our eyes lit up.

"You look beautiful, Ma." I smiled up at her and kissed her cheek

Her black-and-white checked coat had a furry collar and was borrowed from Mrs May in Reading Street; she was about the same size as me Ma. They worked together when Ma was a mechanic. Now they went the market every Saturday in Great Homer Street with Aunty Julia and the three of them were always swapping clothes.

Ma opened her best handbag and fiddled with a pair of black gloves. Around her neck was a small gold crucifix she'd picked up in a second-hand shop. It wasn't real gold, but you wouldn't know.

"You look a treat, Ma," said Cath. And she did.

We set off along Flinders Street and headed up Stanley Road towards the Dock Road. We strolled along the dockside, looking out for me Da's ship. It was nearly Easter and the sun was shining. Everything looked fresh and bright, I said to Ma. "Just like yer own lovely faces," she grinned.

The water sparkled like stars in the night.

We soon clocked Da's ship waiting in the dock, and we headed over to catch him coming down the gangway. Punch's tail began wagging furiously.

"He can smell yer Da before we can even bloody well see him!" said Ma and Punch ran ahead of us. Sure enough, there was me Da at the top of the gangway, his huge kit bag slung over his shoulder.

"Da!" we screamed. "Da! *Da*! Over here."

He spotted us and flew over, dropping his kit to wrap us up in the best hug I've ever had. Me Da was home at last.

Punch squeezed in and almost knocked me Da head over heels into the Mersey.

"No show without Punch, eh, lad?" Da laughed, while Punch washed his face off.

The journey home to Flinders Street was filled with non-stop chatter. Da said he couldn't hear himself think. By the time we reached our front door, Ma had taken her high heels off and stuffed them in her handbag.

"Bloody squashin' me toes! I'll have a pair of pigs' feet in the morning, Jimmy!"

Da laughed. "Get the pan boiling, Emily, and let's all have a nice

*Ma (centre) and the Flinders Street ladies going on a
charabanc trip to Blackpool, with Jimmy White the
accordion player from St. Ollie's.*

cup of tea, eh, me lovely queen," said Da, and Ma's cheeks blushed
pink. "An' how about yer play that piano for me, Emily, after tea, eh?"

Ma smiled and kissed me Da's cheek. "Anythin' in the world for
you, Jimmy. Anythin' at all, luv."

"Then sing us a song, Ma, but never say a long goodbye again."

We spent a few glorious weeks with me Da resting and recuperating
at home. There were plenty of family reunions and celebrations, plenty
of parties with our neighbours, and plenty of barrels rolled out along
Flinders Street. Ma sang and played the piano for me Da until her
fingers blistered; Cath wore her toes out dancing for him. Jimmy read
with him and listened to tales of far-away countries. And I mastered
the ukulele, playing beside him with his harmonica. I practised every
day, even with blistered, bleeding fingers. Da said to soak them in
vinegar, it would toughen the skin up. He was right, as always.

All too soon the dreaded day arrived for Da to return to the
Merchant Navy and pick up his life on the seas – but at least now he
was only away for short periods. We wrote to each other regularly and

enjoyed many a reunion. I missed him so much, but was so proud of him sailing to distant shores, and I loved hearing all about his many adventures. Now I could check the shipping news for the whereabouts of me Da's ship again in the *Liverpool Echo* every week – but we no longer had newspaper tablecloths! Ma had moved up to some posh PVC ones, but she still kept the best silk ones in her china cabinet for Sundays and holidays.

* * * *

Christmas had faded and dwindled into cold January winds. The sleet and snow were almost gone, melted by lukewarm moments of early morning pale yellow sunshine.

My bed was just wide enough for me and Punch to stretch our legs out, though Punch had most of my lumpy pillow. I yawned. Glancing through the gap in my thin brown curtains I could see that the winter sun was already painting the sky a powder blue: my favourite colour.

Kitchen noises swept up the stairs: pots and pans, lids clunking and clanging. Ma's feet shuffled across the kitchen beneath my bedroom. I could hear water pouring from the tap and I knew my morning cup of tea wasn't far away; I'd smell the hot toast in a minute. I ruffled Punch's neck, gently trying to bring him back from the Land of Nod – it was time to get a move on. I nudged him in the ribs.

"Come 'ead Punch," I shook his shoulders. "It's me birthday, Punch! *I'm a bloody teenager today!*"

Cultures like the Native American Indians have understood that without clear markers on the journey into manhood, males have a difficult time making the transition and can drift along indefinitely. Rites of passage were clearly defined as one of the community's most important rituals. There is a huge diversity in what these ceremonies consist of. In 1946 Liverpool, we boys had our own rites of passage, our own ceremony, our own unique transition from boy to man. Saying goodbye to our 'shorties' and pulling on brand-new 'longies', and suddenly the child was gone. Brand-new thoughts and brand-new feelings came with our first taste of adult life. And girls! But falling in love comes with a price...

Ma bellowed up the dancers. "Johnny! Johnny! Come on, birthday boy, yer brekkie's on the table!"

Punch and I took the stairs two at a time and crashed into the kitchen. Ma threw her arms around me and planted big sloppy kisses on my cheek.

"Happy birthday, Johnny luv. Me lovely son's a teenager! Where've all the years gone?"

The kitchen table was brimming with cards and brown paper parcels. A big sponge birthday cake sat in the middle, on top of a bowl.

Cath smiled proudly. "I made yer a cake, soft lad. All by meself, didn't I, Ma?"

"A proper good baker yer are, Cath. Better than me at any rate, luv."

I kissed our Cath on top of her head, which was covered in sausage shaped rags. She slept in them every night so she could have a head full of ringlets. They looked bloody uncomfortable to me.

"Awww thanks Cath," I smiled. "Can't wait to have a slice."

"Not till tonight yer won't. Eat yer breakfast first!" Ma stuck a hand on her hip like a tea-pot.

We scoffed our toast and porridge in next to no time. My eyes never left that big brown parcel tied in string by me Ma's end of the table.

"Come on, Johnny!" Jimmy threw some cards across the table. "Get yer pressies open or we'll be late fer school."

Ma leaned over and passed my present, and smiled.

I fumbled with it, trying to feel what was inside. I didn't have a clue what it could be.

"Come on, get it open!"

I tore open the brown paper with both hands and couldn't believe my eyes when a pair of long, grey trousers fell out.

"You've got me them, Ma! You've got me them!" I flew over to me Ma and squeezed her tight.

"Yer a man now, Johnny," said Cath. "Does that mean yer gonna grow a beard? I don't like beards, Johnny!"

"Noooo Cath, I won't be having a beard, not yet, yer daft head."

"Good" she said. "Wouldn't suit yer anyway"

I was made up with them long grey trousers. No more shorties for me; I was a grown-up man now. Me longies proved it!

"Wait till me mates see them, Ma. They'll be dead jealous, yer know."

Ma laughed. "Well go an' get them on, lad, let's see what yer look like…"

"Come 'ead, Punch!" I called out to my very best friend and we legged it up the dancers.

When I stepped back down, I swaggered like a brand-new man.

CHAPTER 19

A BUCKETFUL OF FIRSTS

Of the footsteps of life,
The friendliness, the strife.
In its beds we have lain,
Youth, love, age and pain.

– E. THOMAS

14 April, 1946

"Where's Mike and Lenny gone?" Bombo Mac picked up the tennis ball. We were having a kick about on the bombed-out site that was once St Aiden's Church. It made a perfect pitch and meeting place.

"They've gone to give Monk Murphy a hand shiftin' an old piano." I wiped the sweat off the back of my neck, glad for a rest. It was roasting hot tonight.

"*Ha*!" said Bombo. "Since when have that pair o' buggers been so helpful! Must be a few bob in piano shiftin' eh, Johnny lad?"

I wandered over to Punch who was supposed to be manning the goal post: two old jumpers and me Da's cap marked it out. Punch was panting, too hot to be our goalie.

"Can yer pass the water please, Bombo? Punch is gaggin'."

He passed over an old jam jar full of lukewarm water. Punch lapped it up out of my hand. I flopped to the ground and stuck my arms behind my head, looking up at the clouds. Bombo collapsed next to me and Punch.

"Bloody hot, isn't it, Johnny?"

Sadie, Joan and Renee were gabbing ten to the dozen over in the corner. I leaned on my elbow clocking what they were up to.

"Why do girls brush each other's hair ,Bombo?"

"God knows, Johnny."

"Maybe they want to be hairdressers?" I suggested.

"Don't know, and don't bloody care."

Bombo was grumpy in the heat. I flung water from the jam jar over his hot head to cool him down and cheer him up.

"Yer've got a face on yer like a slapped kipper, Bombo. Stop whingin' and bloody well buck up!"

Punch jumped up and threw himself on top of Bombo. He burst out laughing, his bad mood disappearing.

"Come 'ead, Johnny, let's have a stroll down the road, see what's goin' on in Lathom Street."

"Yer on, Bombo." I shoved our jumpers under my arm and Punch wrapped his teeth around me Da's old cap. Bombo pocketed the tennis ball and empty jam jar.

The homeless man was still sat in the same dark corner, leaning on the same, half-bricked wall outside what was St Aiden's Church. Sitting on a newspaper and blanket scrap in all weathers he hardly

'Comic swaps' made our day.

felt the cold of the night in winter, he said, without complaint. Still wearing the same threadbare coat, I noticed, even in tonight's heat. It was far too hot to be wearing an overcoat like that. Maybe one of me Da's old, light ones would fit him. *It isn't right, the way he's been treated,* I thought. *I'll ask me Ma after.*

The sunny weather had brought all the kids out in Lathom Street. Bombo booted an old tin can and the dogs rooting in a bin outside one of the big houses scarpered down an entry. A few lads from our class sat on the top step of the dentists swapping football cards.

"Alright Johnny? How's it goin', Bombo? Got any swaps, lads?" Tommy Smith called out.

"Not tonight, lads, we're on a mission," said Bombo.

Hannah and Helen, the red-headed twins from Athol Street, skipped in identical time with identical ropes and identical green dresses. *Two peas in a pod,* said Ma. They were singing something like 'Mary and She' when they whizzed past us not missing a skip or a step; not even bumping into Punch who tried to join in the skip.

"Look at that lot over there, Johnny." A crowd of girls were playing rounders on the bommie.

"Will yer look at the state of the way girls run!" laughed Bombo. "They're about as much use as a chocolate teapot. Those skinny spindly legs look like dead matchsticks to me. Bet they couldn't even outrun a turtle."

"I think you mean a tortoise..."

Bombo cocked his head and frowned.

We hung around and watched the matchstick legs play rounders.

"That's her, Bombo. That's her! She's the one, Bombo, she's the one!"

"Who? What yer on about, soft lad?"

"Who *is* she, Bombo?"

"Who, lad? Who's who?" Bombo Mac looked more bemused than ever.

"That girl, the lovely one with the long legs. D'yer know who she is?"

I pointed to the pretty one, the fastest one, the one with the perfect teeth and long brown hair with curls on the bottom. I'd clocked her first at Sunday Mass in St Ollie's a few weeks back. When I served at the altar with Father Winder, I'd have to hold the communion tray underneath her chin while Father gave her the communion bread. I'd dreamt of her every night since I first clapped eyes on her.

"I 'aven't got a clue, Johnny. I know she doesn't go to our school, though. I think she goes to a posh one 'cos I've spotted her gettin' on the tram into town in a navy and gold uniform. Looks like a bookworm to me, lad. Bet she talks with a mouthful of ollies."

"She's lovely Bombo. I think I'm in love!"

Bombo clouted the back of me head. "Have yer gone bloody daft, lad?"

A pink blur spun past us. "Hiya Johnny!"

I spun round and caught the back of Maureen Ellis racing up the street.

"Where the hell did she spring from, Johnny?" Bombo asked, confused.

"Oh God, she's good at appearing out of nowhere is Maureen Ellis. 'Earwig' we call her in our street. Knows everything about everyone. Like Keyhole Kate in the comics."

We peered up at the eavesdropper. Her fast legs were going ten to the dozen.

"How much did she hear me say, Bombo?"

He shrugged a shoulder and raised one eye. "Yer in for it now, Johnny."

"Eh, Johnny! Johnny!"

Maureen had reached the top of the street and was yelling down at me. "Her name's Nora Kerr," she yelled. "Lives in Snowdrop Street. Number twelve with the brown door!"

Maureen Ellis was gone in a flash.

"Bloody hell, Bombo!" I groaned. "I'll never hear the last of it now. I bet yer it'll be all over our street by tomorrow night. *Everyone* will know I'm in love! What am I gonna do, Bombo?"

Bombo sniffed with not a care in the world and nuzzled into Punch. "Bloody Maureen Ellis and her earwig ears!" I moaned to Bombo and Punch.

I didn't sleep at all well that night.

She was alright, *really*, was Maureen Ellis. When she wasn't nosin' around, anyway. I thought about her the next day, worrying if she'd been gossiping all over the show. 'Nosy Knickers', our Cath called her. Maureen had lived in our street for years, a few doors up from us, and she'd been a good mate for a long time, despite her nosiness.

I was off school as it was a Holy Day of Obligation and I didn't mind at all, not one little bit. "More time to play with you, eh, Punch?" He was made up.

My eyes adjusted to the afternoon sun after stepping out of our dingy, windowless hall. The handles of me Ma's big shopping bag slipped out of my grasp. Shadows pooled in front of me, cast by the ladder propped up outside next door. Mr Moran hovered carefully between two broken wooden rungs, repairing the smashed window upstairs with hardboard.

We were dropping off some veg at Mrs Murphy's so she could make a nice pan of scouse for Monk.

"Johnny! Johnny!" It was Maureen, tugging on me sleeve and out of breath.

"'Ere, Johnny. Yer fancy that Nora one in Snowdrop Street, don't yer, lad?"

"*Shurrup*, Maureen. Don't know what yer talkin' about."

"Yis yer do, Johnny. I know all about it."

My cheeks burned and I looked to my feet, shuffling awkwardly.

"Anyway, Johnny," Maureen was in full swing now she'd got her breath back. "Yer've got a date with her on Friday night. Eight o'clock, Johnny. Don't be late!"

"A date? A date? What yer talkin' about, Maureen? A date with who? I haven't got a date on Friday!"

"Oh yis, yer have. It's all sorted out. Yer goin' out with Nora on Friday night! Get yer best clobber on and get down Snowdrop Street at eight o'clock on Friday. Number twelve, the brown door. Don't be late or she'll kill yer, Johnny!"

Maureen legged it away before I could get another word out.

"I could bloody well kill that Maureen one. What's she gone an' done?" I looked down at Punch, terrified at the thought of a real date. "What the hell am I goin' ter do, Punch? Can yer believe it? A bloody date!"

I couldn't sleep for the next few nights.

A few days later: "God 'elp me," I whispered to Punch on my way out of the door. "Do I look alright, Punch? Will she like me, eh? What am I gonna say to her, Punch? Jesus, Mary an' Joseph, what *am* I doin'?"

Punch stretched out under the easy chair and let out a long yawn.

I set off for my very first date with butterflies in my belly. My knees were like jelly. I thought I was going to be sick. The bells started ringing as soon as I rounded the corner into Snowdrop Street. The bells in my head. And a clanking noise in the pit of my belly. Like a ghost dragging heavy chains. I forced my legs to keep moving forward. One step at a time, like walking through treacle. Never in my life had I felt this animal inside me. Sleek, full-bodied, ready to burst out in nervous laughter like a panther. And I couldn't wipe the silly smile off my face. My cheek muscles fixed in a grin.

A salty, seaweedy kind of smell filled the air, probably dragged off the Mersey by the warm wind. The sun shone bright and lit up all the houses. Someone pushed a pram on the other side of the street, a baby's gurgles that could have been a song.

Johnny's sweetheart from
Snowdrop Street, Nora Kerr.

Frank Sinatra sang out as I passed by an open window. "*Five minutes more...*" he crooned – and suddenly she appeared. Her blue dress swung with each long-legged stride. Pony-tailed hair glistened in the rays of a golden sun.

"I love this song, Johnny, don't you?"

That smoky, husky voice did it. The perfect teeth did it. Everything about her was perfect. Frozen in time, I knew it was the moment I'd found the love of my life.

* * * *

The beautiful warm evening saw us strolling through the streets of Liverpool. The grim brick wall on one side of Melrose Road seemed to stretch for miles, backing on to the railway line that ran past Bootle and north of the docks. Identical terraced streets lined up opposite the long blank wall. The houses looked weary after the War; like other streets they all needed cheering up. We covered miles, walking hand-in-hand beneath the overhead railway called the Docker's Umbrella, on the Dock Road, waving to passengers on their way into the south end of Liverpool. We chatted never-endingly outside Tate and Lyles on the perfectly named Love Lane, like we'd known each other forever. The smell of crystalized sugar mingled sweetly amonst our laughter. We skipped further up through the streets to the B.A.T. factory and the heady aroma of tobacco leaves filled our head with a dizzy lightness. Love's first awakening would never sleep again.

All too soon, a fading sun's pink beams became a pale moonlit sky, glittering softly on Nora's glossy hair. We danced right there, under the clock outside the tobacco factory in our very own secret spot.

"This will be *our* special place, Johnny," Nora whispered huskily into my ear.

"*Forever*," I whispered back. Nora patiently showed me how to waltz with my two left feet. Humming quietly we twirled in perfect time on that empty street where we first fell in love.

We headed back down Snowdrop Street, floating on air.

I dared to kiss her pretty pink lips outside her front door.

"Goodnight, sweetheart," I croaked.

"See you tomorrow, Johnny, outside our clock. Don't be late."

I would never be late for Nora. Not once, not ever.

I danced all the way back home to Flinders Street and stopped underneath the lamppost. Looking up at a huge, full, bright moon I made a life-long promise.

"I promise you, God, I will love Nora forever." I meant it. Ma taught me to never make a promise I couldn't keep.

I'd love my Sweetheart from Snowdrop Street forever.

* * * *

She always stood out from the crowd; her college uniform was always neat and crisp – not a wrinkle in sight on a snow-white shirt. Her gold and navy blue tie held a perfect Windsor knot. Her hat was perched at just the right angle, a long silk ribbon touching a small ear. A pair of long legs that ran quickly and furiously, winning school races easily, she was captain of the rounders and hockey team and she gave many a run for their money in netball. When we met she'd recently moved from a flat a few miles away by St Paul's Eye Hospital, not far from the Pier Head; her family had found a bigger house in Snowdrop Street. Nora never said much when in a crowd, but her sharp brain never missed a trick and she used to quietly observe the goings-on around her. She carried stacks of books in a brown leather satchel, lugging them on to the tram ride home from school each night. She loved being top of the class in her posh Catholic School: Broughton Hall College in West Derby, by Alder Hey Children's Hospital. *One day,* she had vowed, *I will be a headmistress and pass on great knowledge.* I never doubted her commitment for a second.

* * * *

It was the summer of 1947 when I hopped on to the number 16 tram at seven o'clock on Monday morning. Sitting in the middle row was Jackie, an old friend from my primary school, Daisy Street.

"Yer look as white as a sheet, Johnny, what's up wi' yer, mate?"

Nora and I had danced and laughed through our blossoming courtship: celebrating our first Christmas together, our first birthdays, our first jobs.

Now, as I explained to Jackie, it was my first day in my first proper job. I'd managed to find work in the loading bay at Hayes and Finch, candle-makers who supplied every Catholic Church in Britain. I would be trucking large bags of old wax candles from the loading bay and up to the third floor. The old wax would be tipped into huge vats of melting wax. I'd already been shown around the factory when I was interviewed. The massive vats looked dangerous, the lighting so dim you could hardly see three feet in front of yerself!

Party Time in Flinders Street.

"Be bloody careful, Johnny!" warned Ma and Nora.

I walked through the doors of Hayes and Finch shaking from head to toe. An old guy with wispy, silvery hair met me outside the office and said he would kit me out with my overalls. His own pair were splattered with patches of hardened wax. I wondered if it would ever come off. His sunken, hollow cheeks made his yellow teeth look far too big for his head. I reckoned he was at least a hundred years old.

"I'm Moriarty," he croaked. "An' I'll be showin' yer around this place, tellin' yer what's what, like. But I'm warnin' yer, take no notice of the gossip, lad. I don't eat up all the new lads or throw them in the vat for the waxworks. Well, maybe not all of them." I wasn't quite sure. And with a name like Moriarty, I did think he had a bit of a look of Sherlock Holmes arch enemy.

I was made up at dinnertime. Me and a few of the other young lads were able to play football on the large field next to the factory. It made the ideal pitch so I could get in a bit of footie practise now that I was playing for a local team, St Albans.

I couldn't wait for my first week's wages. Twenty-five shillings! The first thing I would do was take Nora to the pictures. *The Al Jolson Story* was showing at the Liverpool Odeon on London Road,

A taste of freedom following the long years of war.

the biggest and best cinema in Liverpool. The next thing I would do is book myself some guitar lessons. I'd found a teacher in Lark Lane, in the south end of Liverpool. Eric Parr would give me weekly lessons for five shillings. Me and a few mates were going to start up a group and play in the pubs along Scotland Road and the Dock Road. Our Jimmy was working at the docks now. He planned to learn all he could about the shipping industry and work his way up to shipping manager in Customs and Excise. Our Cath was still singing and dancing her legs off and planned to join a dance troupe and go on the stage. I didn't doubt for a second that my brother and sister would live their dreams.

Nora, too, had started her own job in the British Telephone Company in Liverpool's town centre. She was a clerical worker and operated the switchboard while she took evening classes for her teaching exams. When the timings worked out we could even travel to work together on the number 16 tram.

CHAPTER 20

DON'T LET THE STARS
GET IN YOUR EYES

12 February, 1954

My courtship with Nora grew strong. I loved her as much as I did the first time I ever saw her.

Over the years, Da and Nora had encouraged me to find new work with greater prospects.

"Get a trade under yer belt," said Da," yer can't go wrong with a trade, son."

Nora had helped me secure an apprenticeship as an electrician; life was busy and full. I had, as I promised myself I would, mastered the guitar. The draw of being in a Country and Western band was as strong as ever. I teamed up with my mate Mike and we had vowed that when we got good enough we'd play country songs in the pubs along the Dock Road and Scotland Road. Hank Williams and Jimmy Rodgers were my greatest influence, my desire to make a record was still a big and distant dream.

My other great love was football. I still played for my local team, still went to every footie practise and vowed to never miss an Everton home match, ever. The days and nights rolled into years as my work, music and football consumed me.

On the international stage, and in the background, catastrophic British defeats in Europe and Asia between 1940 and 1942 had destroyed the country's financial and economic independence, the foundation of imperialism. It had erased the balance of power on which British security had largely depended.

Although Britain was one of the victorious allies, the defeat of

Germany had been mainly the work of Soviet and American power, while that of Japan had been an almost entirely American triumph. So Britain had survived and recovered the territory lost during the War, but its prestige and authority and wealth had been severely reduced. In a bid to win Congress support from India, Britain had promised to give the country full independence once the War was over. Despite British hopes of keeping India united, it became clear that Partition was inevitable and Mountbatten staged a rapid handover to two successor governments, India and Pakistan, almost before the ink was dry on their post-imperial frontiers. With the collapse of imperial power, British leaders came quickly to realise that the country's recovery would take time. Britain rolled into a new decade while the world changed – new dreams were being born, new ideas blossomed, and hope inspired movement to flourish.

Liverpool, too, was making its post-War recovery. A massive slum clearance had begun in earnest and the city was taking on a whole new face. The war-damaged buildings were being replaced and new developments were cropping up. People were spending more even though rationing didn't end until 1954. Low cost housing sprung up around the country; more and more people were beginning to own cars and televisions. Teddy Boys and Rock and Roll brought a sense of freedom after so many years of fear and austerity.

As the recovery continued, so my love for Nora had grown and deepened as the years passed by in the hazy warmth of love's young dream. We loved, we laughed; if only we had never grown up. If only time could've stood still.

Somehow, things began to change.

Somehow, she didn't seem herself these days.

Granted, I didn't see her as often, what with my playing in the pubs and football. Our uncomfortable silences got longer, though I wasn't quite sure why. Coming home one night from the Grosvenor Cinema we had a conversation that would stay with me forever.

"Do you love me, Johnny?"

"Course I do, Nora"

"Will you love me forever?"

"Forever Nora. Forever and a day."

We kissed and I spun her around in my arms.

"Do you love me more than your guitar? More than your footy?"

"Don't be daft, course I do!"

"Are you sure?"

Perhaps I paused a moment too long.

"I think we need some time to think about what we *really* want," said Nora, "and whether or not we have a future together." We held hands and avoided each other's eyes.

"Meet me at our clock on Friday," she said. "Same time as usual. If you don't show up then I'll know you *really* want to say goodbye and do other things, like your guitar and footy," Norah cried, and I couldn't understand what was happening.

"I love you, Nora. I *will* be there for you, sweetheart!"

"Have a *good* think about it Johnny, ask your heart. And I'll ask mine."

"If *you* don't show up, Nora, I'll know it's *you* that really wants to say goodbye," I said sadly, and we parted, unsmiling.

"Till Friday," I called out, but I wasn't sure if she heard me. A tear spilled off my nose. I didn't understand what was happening to us.

On Friday, I stood at our special place at the usual time. The big clock struck loudly. I positioned myself so I could spot the tram easily from a distance. This was the exact same spot where we first fell in love all those years ago. The same spot we first kissed. The same spot we first danced. The same spot we first giggled. I'd been up the last few nights worrying, thinking, remembering.

Waiting at our clock I was terrified. A cold wind and nerves ran down my back. I didn't want us to say goodbye. Not now; not ever. I loved her. With all my heart I loved her. My guitar and football didn't even come a close second. Not really. I'd been a fool, I'd made her feel second best. I hadn't given enough of my time. I could see that now.

I looked up at the clock. The fingers moved painfully slowly. I craned my neck, searching for the number 16 tram. *Five minutes more,* Frank Sinatra sang in my head, again. *Our song.*

I felt as sick as a dog. Please God, don't let me lose her. Not now.

I clocked the tram, rumbling towards me as if in slow motion. As people bustled off, I heard a familiar voice.

"Hiya, Johnny. Waitin' for me are yer, lad?"

It was Bombo Mac. "Oh, it's you," I mumbled miserably. He ran up the road, *late again for somewhere,* I imagined.

"Eh, Johnny luv, you look smart!. Goin' anywhere nice are yer?"

Aunty Julia hopped off the tram and kissed my cheek. "I might be, Aunty Julia. All depends, really."

"Well, see yer later, luv. Have a nice time wherever yer end up. Ta-ra, luv."

I searched the crowd getting off the tram. A tall lady in a green coat with a fur collar and a matching hat was next, but no sign of Nora. The tram emptied and I watched it disappear into the bleak distance on that cold night of misery.

I had waited, but all I heard was silence. I took it as her answer. Nora had said her last goodbye without any words.

That long, lonely journey home on that awful night – which would haunt me forever – felt like a lifetime.

I flung myself on my bed, sobbing my heart out to Punch who was lying beside me. *"What'll I do, Punch?"* He could offer no answers except give me a loving nuzzle from his warm, wet nose. *"Where do I go from here?"*

I squashed up close beside Punch and cried a bucketful of tears on that, the first of many nights of tears and regrets.

The heartache I felt was no less than a bereavement; the devastation was absolute. When I searched inside myself what was left was open and raw; but with help it would remain a solid foundation on which to one day build a new life. But not yet.

I will be wiser one day, I said to myself. *I will know then for whom the doors are open and for whom they must stay locked.* Till another time? I didn't yet have the answers.

I prayed there were more dreams to come for Nora and I. Sunshine on rainy days, laughter and silliness. Now though, I had to somehow endure my loss and grow from it.

When I look back to times gone by
There is one sure thing I know
It is you my love, who stole my heart,
Over fifty years ago.

   – R. N. COOK

CHAPTER 21

THERE MUST BE A REASON

"My battle dress blouse fitted me perfectly. So the quarter-master Sergeant apologised and assured me it didn't usually happen..."

10 September, 1954

I rushed down the bare wooden stairs in Flinders Street in my polished, best black shoes. I didn't want to get any smears on them, not today. Our Jimmy bulled them up to a mirror shine late into the night. "Yer'll soon be spit 'n' bullin' your own shoes and boots, Johnny," he smirked. "The army has yer bullin' every bloody day!"

Wartime conscription had been extended into an obligatory period of National Service for men of military age. More than two million were called up to the armed forces, often serving in one of Britain's many garrisons around the world. The conscripts were given six weeks of basic training, and were knocked into shape by sergeants under pressure to train them in as short a time as possible. Some found it awful; others found it a time of great camaraderie.

Recruits began a strict daily regime, often featuring the seemingly endless polishing of kit. Many saw it as a mindless drill aimed at destroying individuality. The discipline, however, was geared to help nurture a team identity and bring the men closer together. Bonds were cemented between men whose backgrounds were poles apart and who were thrown together in strange new situations. Those bonds grew and were deepened by the discipline thrust upon them. Friendships were strengthened and would last a lifetime for many. There were endless drills, gruelling inspections, physical training, rifle practise. The sergeants and corporals shouted and swore from dawn till dusk; the uniforms mostly didn't fit. Cold barracks. Primitive toilets. Some recruits were housed in 'Barrack Spiders' – wooden huts with eight rooms and a washing area, twenty men to a room. Steel wardrobes and iron beds had a one-foot square locker for small kit.

Most recruits couldn't wait to be discharged after two years of service. But when demob day finally did arrive you'd often hear them whisper with a lump in their throat, *"Christ, I'm going to miss you guys."*

On this, the day I was called up, the steel grey hands of my Timex watch showed ten-fifteen. Time was running away.

Ma had bagged me the bargain watch in Lemon Street, at her favourite second-hand shop. "It was a giveaway, luv." Ma was made up with herself. "I think it used to be that old Mr Riley's – d'ya know who I mean, luv? That grumpy old sod on Stanley Road? The one with not a tooth in his head and bald as a billiard ball? Had that scruffy fish shop by the hospital?"

"I know the fella yer mean, Ma."

"God, he didn't half stink to high heaven, and never had a good word for anyone. Anyway, he was found dead in his bed a couple of weeks ago. God rest his soul. Mind you luv, he *was* ninety-two."

I grinned and gave Ma a wink. "It's a great watch Ma, thank you." The leather strap was a bit worn but that didn't matter.

"Eh, I'll look all posh, wont I, Ma?" I checked the time. Ten-thirty.

"Well," said Ma, "I thought you'll be needing a watch what with catchin' trains an' buses all over the show. Yer wouldn't want to be late, would yer, son? Not with yer National Service."

"I won't be late, Ma, or the Sergeant will likely kill me!" I winked. "I've heard all about them bloody sergeants."

"I'll show them the back of me hand as big as they are if they go upsettin' my son! Bloody sergeants? Wait till they see yer mother!"

We burst out laughing and I leaned down to ruffle me Ma's hair. Punch almost trod on my shoe. I stroked the top of his head, the snowy bit that stuck up like a turkey cock.

I watched him closely. Hobbling slowly around our kitchen with his nose down, sniffing out an odd crumb or two. He was aging now. A little deaf in the right ear; a little blind in the left eye. His once glossy chestnut brown coat turned salt and pepper last winter.

But Punch's tail still wagged, and he sat waiting behind our front door every night till I got home from work. And he loved that daily dose of cod liver oil on a big silver soup spoon. "To oil yer little legs and take away yer aches," Ma smiled, when Punch lapped it up.

"Bloody hell" Aunty Julia hooted, "how in God's name can anyone love bloody cod liver oil?"

Me and Punch wandered into the living room and joined our Cath. I checked my watch again. I looked at my letter again, the one that came a couple of weeks ago. I'd hardly slept a real wink since. I'd been called up. Conscripted into the bloody Army!

"I'll be gone for two bloody years!" I shouted over to our Cath from the easy chair, but she ignored me. I'd been whinging the same thing every day for the last two weeks.

"Change the record," she mumbled under her breath, and carried on sticking a hundred clips in her hair. "I'm making kiss curls, Johnny," she told me when I asked what she was doing to her head. "Wait till yer see me when it's done. I'll be as curly as a savoy cabbage." It looked complicated and painful to me.

"I'm dancing with Renee tonight," she said excitedly. "There's a competition at Blair Hall. I'm always lucky in that place, must be a bit of magic in Walton." I watched as she wound lengths of hair around her fingers then secured it with two crossed clips in an *x* shape.

"Anyway, Johnny," she said matter-of-factly, "two years will fly by! Yer'll be back before you're gone."

"I bet yer win first prize tonight, Cath," I said, as she shuffled her feet in some kind of fancy dance move. "Yer've always been a proper little Dancing Queen. Better than Ginger Rogers. Yer were *born* to dance, Cath. Don't think you'd ever me able to teach me, though, I'm a lost cause on me toes."

"Awww, thanks, soft lad. An' it's only because of your two left feet. Besides, you can make a guitar sing, Johnny. Everyone's got a talent somewhere. Look at our Jimmy on his drums, and me Ma on her piano. Aunty Julia's got a smashing singing voice and me Da's fantastic with his harmonica."

She leaned over and planted a kiss on my cheek. She glanced up at the mirror above the fireplace. She had an innocent beauty even without a trace of make-up on, and a head full of peculiar clips. "*Ain't that a shame*," she sung at the top of her voice.

"It is a shame, Cath. A bloody shame indeed! I still can't believe I'm being carted off for two whole years! Feels like a bloody prison sentence."

"It's *not* a prison, soft lad!" Cath hooted.

"You'll have a great time at the barracks. Loads of new mates and adventures, just you wait and see." She twirled off, bounced out of the door and up the dancers, preening herself.

I looked down at my watch. Eleven-thirty. Cath stopped on the halfway stair and stuck her head through the bannister railings.

"Oy, soft lad! What time's yer train leavin'? You've been clockin' that watch all bloody mornin'!"

"Six o'clock tonight," I yelled through the half open door.

"Oh, yer've loads of time left! Make the most of *every minute of now!* It's all any one of us has got, really. Make the most of now!"

She flew up to her room singing "*You're in the army now...*"

A soft light and quietness fell in the living room and I sat back in the easy chair drifting and dreaming. A weak bit of yellow sunshine streamed through the freshly cleaned window which still smelt of vinegar.

Cath's words struck me. Make the most of now, she'd said. It's all any one of us has got. *She's right*, I thought. *No good me sittin' here mopin'! I should take Punch out and say ta-ra to me mates.*

"Come 'ead, Punch, let's see what we can find in the streets."
I glanced back along our hall and into the kitchen where Ma was
struggling and cursing under her breath. Folding up a striped fleecy
bed sheet she was all in a frustrated twist. I grabbed one end of the
candy-striped, worn-out sheet,
    " 'Ere, Ma, let me give a hand before I see me mates."
    "Awww, thanks luv. They'd tangle the life out of a parrot."
    Soon as Ma was sorted we were ready to wander through Kirkdale.
    "Ta-ra Ma, see yer in a bit!" I shouted from the front door.
    "Don't be late! Check yer watch!"
    "Yis, Ma."
    Me and Punch strolled along all our favourite streets and bid farewell
to a few old mates. A lot of them were gone too, away doing their
own National Service either in the Army or the Navy. Some of them
were serving as regulars. Old friends scattered across the country and
abroad. But a few were on home leave, like Bombo Mac, Lenny and
Tony. We had a quick game of footie and I thanked God I'd changed
out of my best shoes. I checked my watch and headed back home.

* * * *

It's a heart-breaking and painful moment waving goodbye to the safe
and familiar constants in your life and embracing new adventures.
Leaving home for the first time. Flying the nest. You feel as if a part
of you is being torn away. You are used to relying on each other for
everything; every decision from the smallest to the largest is made
with the consultation of your family, you have known no other way.
When you are separated, you must accustom yourself to living single,
you don't have that constant reassurance of having someone to lean
on. This feeling takes time to get used to.
    They all came to say goodbye on the day I left for my National
Service. Gathered on the doorstep of Flinders Street. Me Ma, Aunty

Julia, our Jimmy and Cath and my best friend, Punch, with Judy, of course. And all the neighbours. My heart left my mouth.

I crouched down on my knees and pulled Punch close to me

"Now listen, Punch," He looked up at me earnestly with his moist, caramel eyes, head cocked on his non-deaf side. "Cath will carry you up to bed each night, you'll be sleeping with her for now, just till I'm back. You'll like it in Cath's bed, it's nice and soft."

Cath knelt down and stroked Punch too.

"You'll be spoilt rotten, won't yer Punch? Treat you like a king, we will."

I just couldn't swallow that lump in my throat.

"I love you, Punch, my dear old friend. I'll be back, I promise I will."

I dragged myself away and on the corner of the street I gave my final wave and blew a last kiss to Punch and me Ma.

Jimmy in Somalia 1948 doing his National Service.

There was a cold chill in the air as I shuffled across town to board that train; the first stirrings of Autumn. Lizzie the flower-seller was in her usual spot by Central Station, clutching a big bunch of pink carnations and singing 'I See the Moon'. I decided there and then that I would buy my Ma those pretty flowers she'd always longed for when I come home on my first leave.

I crouched down to tie my shoelace; the jacket of my suit was open and blew behind me, tangling up with my kit bag. I noticed some stray white hairs from Punch stuck on my black shiny shoes and I left them there, no longer bothered if my shoes got smeared. I carried on up Bold Street with a heavy heart.

Town was full of Teddy Boys and Girls, heading for a quick drink in Yates' Wine Lodge. Some had joined the long queue outside the Futurist Cinema. I pushed through shoppers still gazing in shop windows. I hardly noticed the young people out for the night, couples with arms linked, smoking, chatting. Nonsensical noise buzzed in my ears.

There was music drifting through the air. For as long as I had been coming to Bold Street there was always music playing somewhere in this busy street. It could have been Mr Sainsbury who lived in our street and played the accordion and sang for a living. Or it could have been old Joe McGuire who had a taste for whiskey and usually wobbled outside Cramer and Lea, the music shop where I bought my first guitar. Joe was doing his best to play an out-of-tune banjo with the only two chords he knew. He couldn't sing for toffee but that never stopped him. He lived in our street, too.

Lime Street Station was almost in sight. That lump was still in my throat.

"Johnny! Johnny!"

I thought I heard my name but didn't look up. Must be someone else, I carried on dragging my heels.

"Johnny!"

"Oy! Soft lad!"

Cath's dancing partners, 'The Teddy Boys'.

I knew that voice! I whipped round quick.

Our Cath was flying up the road, her dancing feet going twenty to the dozen.

"Yer've forgot yer hat, soft lad!"

I caught my hat mid-air and laughed.

"Yer better not have made me late for me dance competition, Johnny!"

She smiled and turned around, calling over her shoulder. "What d'yer think of me latest moves? Will I win tonight?"

"First prize, Cath!" I shouted as loud as I could.

She twirled and whirled, dancing her legs off back down the street, singing at the top of her sweet voice, *"Ain't that a shame…"* I smiled at my Dancing Queen Sister.

I would never see her dance again.

* * * *

It was by no means the Ritz. My new home didn't even come close to a lodging house for cats.

"By the left, quick MARCH!" The Sergeant bellowed like a fog horn. Bloody parades; square-bashing for England. I was sweating cobs in another quick march before I collapsed in the heat. It made no odds that it was cold, grey and peeing down, I was as roasting hot as if the sun was cracking the flags. I hated parades and fainted more than once. It was carrying all that heavy kit that did it. My feet were blistered to high heaven. The blisters from last week hadn't healed yet and here was another fresh bunch weeping, sticking to my socks. I winced each night picking them off, like rubbing salt in open wound.

The sergeant swore one more time. Well, why would he stop? He'd been at it all day.

"How many more weeks have we got left of training?" I whispered out of the corner of my mouth to the skinny lad with tiny feet and trousers halfway up his legs.

"Private Slater, shurrup! On yer belly now! Twenty push-ups!"

God, that'll teach me to keep my mouth shut. I almost threw up last night's sausage and mash. The only reason it stayed in my belly was because I was half-starved. My belly hung on to what little was in it. The sausage could have been used to sole your shoes and the mash was more like wallpaper paste. You could have varnished the door with the burnt-orange, cold, mug of tea.

"Elbows straight, Private Slater! You can bull your lazy mates' boots after, for shirking like a wet nelly."

I groaned and felt tears sting my eyes. I wanted to go home! I thought that drowning must be a terrible death, but this was far worse. *I should have joined the RAF,* I thought. *I bet they treat you better than this.*

But we got through it. By the skin of our teeth, we survived the God-awful training, that I'll never in a million years forget.

We joined up as boys and after two long years, we came out as men.

Except, perhaps the Drag Queen who may have found his true calling on the night of our Christmas show…

* * * *

It was Christmas, 1955. Corporal Bonner legged it over to the N.A.F.F.I. canteen, head down against the shower of wet grey snow. His boots clanked heavily up the metal steps. He burst through the door, shaking his neck to rid himself of the dissolving flakes of mushy sleet. At least the hailstones had gone.

"Don't touch my drums!" he yelled across the large hall to the cleaner who thought she was doing him a favour by shining his cymbals. Mince pies and Christmas puddings smelt fruity, oranges and cloves much better than the usual cabbage and boiled spuds.

The show for Christmas was going to be a cracker. Singers, comedians, magicians, we had the lot.

The Drag Queen flirted across the mock-up stage in a white silk, low-cut dress. What he had used for his overly large breasts was anyone's guess. Preening elegantly in a pair of too-small red stilettos you wouldn't have been mistaken in thinking he'd done this before. He was a dead ringer for Marylin Monroe, especially the swing of his hips. Batting black mascared eyes he pouted those cherry-red lips and blew kisses to the lads. The audience didn't realise at first that he was actually a bloke, and they went wild. Marylin brought the house down – yet we never did get to know exactly which Private he was!

I did a turn on my guitar with Corporal Bonner on drums, the Welsh lad Taff on the piano, and Dick Rigby sang his heart out to Frankie Lane's 'Frankie and Johnny' and 'Lucky Old Star'. It was my first and last experience of wearing make-up. It took me all bloody night to get the muck off.

Letters from me Ma and Aunty Julia at home kept me going. Ma sent me a fruitcake once but when it arrived it looked more like last week's breadcrumbs. It would have been better in a tin and not a brown paper bag.

The barracks were just about wide enough for the eight of us to stand up and lie down. Our metal beds were rigid, and lined up in perfect order. The cold walls were made from brick, and damp. A few small windows offered no view except for the grey, grimy stone surface of the parade ground.

Bill, the bloke from Glasgow, perched on his own bed opposite mine and the rest of our barrack mates gathered around, ready to help Bill out with another favour. By his own admittance he couldn't string a sentence together. His sweetheart back home in Glasgow, Maggie McQueen, wanted him to write to her twice a week. So twice a week the eight of us sat back on our beds and composed love letters to Maggie on behalf of Bill. And we went to town on those love letters. Romeo himself couldn't have done a better job. We screamed laughing, wondering if his secret would stay safe.

* * * *

I received my posting to Hamburg and tasted my first trip abroad. Germany in the 1950s was being reconstructed quickly, far more so than Britain. Rationing in Britain was still a very recent memory but eating out in Germany was a real treat. Fruit cakes smothered in delicious cream were a firm favourite of mine. Few of us conscripts spoke the language but on the whole people were friendly, though we didn't really mix with the locals. We learnt enough to get by. Certain privileges were still available – fuel concessions – and within the barracks, drink and tobacco were much cheaper, while consumer goods were in abundance, unlike Britain.

But – I still missed Nora so much. Not a day went by when I wasn't yearning for my lost love. I carried my heartache with me and in the lonely, empty hours I still wept for a true love lost. I put on a brave front, though, and embraced my new adventure in Germany as best I could, little knowing how suddenly it all could all change.

CHAPTER 22

THE LONGEST JOURNEY

2 February, 1956

We roamed across the spotless parade ground, heading for the canteen, the promise of a Sunday morning breakfast tantalizing our taste buds. Best brekkie of the week. My cheeks reddened with the warm, early morning sunshine and Germanys fresh crisp air.

"Are you having fried eggs, Johnny, or bacon and beans?" asked Eric, the six foot two Birmingham lad who acted daft when it suited him.

"I'm havin' the bloody lot, Eric, second helpings too. I'm starvin'!"

"You're always starving, Johnny; your belly's a bottomless pit, mate!"

We were almost at the canteen's wooden doors when a voice rang out of the Tannoy.

"Corporal Slater! Corporal Slater! To the guardhouse, now!"

I stopped in my tracks, mortified. Eric did, too, and we stared at each other, dumbfounded.

"My God, Johnny, what have you done, mate?" Eric swivelled towards me, turning a pale shade of white – but not as pale as me.

"Jesus, Mary and Joseph, I have no idea, Eric!"

"Get a move on, Johnny. Must be something bad mate, it's a bloody Sunday morning!"

I legged it over to the guardhouse. What the hell had I done? I knocked quietly on the small glass pane and swallowed a ball of fear. I was surprised to see the door opening without hearing the usual command, "Enter!"

Duty Corporal Hunt gripped my shoulder and slowly led me inside.

"Come and sit down, Johnny, son". It was almost a whisper. His soft West Country accent wasn't normally soft at all. He pulled out a large, wooden chair and nudged me slowly into it. Sitting beside me he put his large, weathered hand on my shoulder.

I glanced around the guardhouse and stared at the dusty clock above his desk. Eight-fifteen.

The guardhouse was in perfect order. The Bristol Corporal was a stickler for tidiness, insisting everything had its own home, its own place. Neat stacks of books and scribbled notes lined up in perfect uniform on his dust free desk. Small framed pictures of Officers and military certificates arranged in perfect symmetry across three, pale blue walls. Muffled voices drifted through the slightly open window behind me.

"What am I doing here?" I asked. "What's going on?" And I wondered why Corporal Hunt was looking at me like that.

He leaned towards me, his hand still on my left shoulder. His pale green eyes looked sorrowful.

"I am so sorry, Johnny. I have to be the bearer of some terrible, tragic news, son."

He took a large gulp and I sat there speechless, frozen to the chair.

"There's been an awful accident in Liverpool. It's your sister, Cath. She's been killed in an accident. I'm so sorry."

"*Cath!*" I screamed. "Our Cath? *Killed?*" Corporal Hunt jumped up and held on to me, as I sobbed in his rough, uniformed arms.

"How can my sister be dead? *How?* How can our Cath be dead? It can't be true! She's only nineteen, for God's sake. *How?*"

Corporal Hunt flung open the door, yelling for someone to grab me a strong cup of tea. "And fill it up with brandy!" he ordered. My mind had gone numb. I was shaking all over.

"*How, how?*"

I sobbed and sobbed, trying to get the words out.

"It was a road accident. An awful, awful road accident. Your sister had been out for the night at the pictures with her friend. They were on a zebra crossing when a bus went out of control. Your sister pushed her friend to safety but sadly the bus hit your Cath. It was instant, son, she wouldn't have known anything. She saved the life of her best friend. She put the life of another before herself, son. Her last act of kindness was the bravest thing any soul could ever do. Be very proud of her. She must have been a wonderful sister. I'm so sorry, son. There's nothing I can say to ease your pain right now but I promise you, we are all here for you, and we will do *anything* to get you back home to your family as soon as possible."

He shoved a cup of brandy laced tea in my hand. "Drink that right back, now."

They were all so kind to me at the barracks. The sergeants, the corporals, the privates, my mates. I wasn't left on my own for a minute. I remained in a fog of sorrow and shock. Raw, weary, and bruised to the bone. Shattered at the loss of a beloved sister who no-one would ever see dance again. And horrified at the irony of her surviving a war only to be taken by a careless bus driver. It was so very wrong, a young life so cruelly torn away.

It was going to take me three days to travel back home to Liverpool via boats and trains. A long, lonely journey. No-one at the barracks was happy sending me off on such an awful trip. In the end, they all pooled together and had a whip-round for a single plane ticket to Heathrow, landing early on the morning of Cath's funeral. I can never thank those lads enough for easing that awful journey.

I boarded the train from London to Liverpool, yet I have no memory of how I got there.

With the dim light filtering through a film of ash and oil on the plate glass roof of Lime Street Station, I shouldered my kit-bag and sighed. I shuffled across the dirty, grey platform in my best shoes and dress uniform for Cath's funeral. I avoided eye contact with the seething mass of humanity. I detected a smell of lost hope mingling with the steam from the trains' engines. The huge clock ticked mournfully. And there in the entrance they stood, lost and lonely. My family, torn and broken. I squared my shoulders and swallowed the bitter tears threating to choke me.

I saw Ma. The tears flowed silently down her cheeks, dripping on to the cold ground of Lime Street Station. She was too sad to cry out or wail. She just stood there, while the magnitude of her loss swept over her. When asked, years later, to describe her sadness in the moment she heard of the tragic news of her daughter's death, her eyes would brim with tears once more, as if the years had passed in a matter of seconds and she could say nothing, lost forever in the terrible emptiness of that moment. It was a moment that carried her forwards until only death could release her from its clutches. She was forever tormented by a past that could not be undone.

Da looked dreadful. Haunted. Like he'd aged at least twenty years. Broken, he stood lost and lonely. He wrapped me up in a gut-wrenching hug, sobbing. His sagging shoulders shook with mine and together we ached for his young daughter and my beloved sister, now lost to us. We had spoken and cried so many tears over the last few days, Ma, Da, me and our Jimmy. Painful, unimaginable phone calls back and forth across the bleak North Sea, from the guardhouse in Germany to the only phone owner we knew – Mrs Kelly and her black phone in Flinders Street.

Jimmy's face was a grey-white against his new black suit. His sunken cheeks were hollow, his lips pinched, anaemic. His usually sparkly blue eyes were empty, except for tears swimming along his bottom lids. His large, tanned hands, not knowing what to do with themselves, fluttered and flapped. He cried bitter tears and asked, of no-one in particular, "*Why? Why?*"

My childhood friend, Frankie, had driven my family over to Lime Street Station and he would take us all to St Alphonsus' church in Great Mersey Street. Frankie wept buckets as we trudged over to his waiting car. Somehow we made that dreadful drive, to our Cath's funeral.

We drew up slowly outside the beautiful, old stone church of St Alphonsus. The glorious stained-glass windows glistened in the rays of a weak sunshine. My eyes took in the hundreds of people lined up in their very best clothes. They had all come to say goodbye to our Cath. Hundreds more spilled on to the streets, stretching all the way down to Kirkdale Road. There must have been a thousand faces.

I heard someone whisper, "*Cath would be made up seeing Johnny in his uniform. She always said how smart he looked.*"

I spotted Lilly Longshanks, her eyes huge and puffy-red. Her shaky hand held a hanky to her cheek, dabbing her sad face underneath a small, black felt hat. Sobs rippled throughout the graveyard. Ma and Da could hardly stand upright, propped up by our Jimmy on one side and Aunty Julia on the other. They looked small and weak, probably from crying day and night since hearing the tragic news. I could see how difficult it was for the pair of them to keep everything together, for the sake of everyone else.

Granny Murphy stood staring straight ahead at Father Winder in the doorway. Bloodshot lines added to her already tired, worn out face. Her shoulders drooped and she looked so much smaller today.

Father Winder stood tall and graceful, a vibrant purple stole draped over his pure white robe. At the centre of the alter he stood solemn, ready to conduct Cath's Requiem Mass. Myrrh and Frankincense, pungent and pure, wafted through every crevice in that crammed, small church in the corner of Kirkdale.

"Today," Father Winder began, "We say goodbye to our beloved Cath...".

The sobs broke free, unchecked by none.

Her coffin sank slowly into the ground. Yellow and white flowers for our Dancing Queen. Ma sobbed, her knees collapsing as she fell into Da's trembling arms. I couldn't bear to look, their pain far too raw and deep. I glimpsed over at our Jimmy whose chin trembled as much as his shoulders. *God help me, if only I could do something, anything, to make them all feel better.*

Ma and Da's whispers came in stifled gasps between clenched lips. "*Goodbye, our Cath,*" they said softly, clinging tightly to each before tossing two perfect yellow roses for Cath to take with her. An abundance of fresh flowers surrounded the grave, a gift from kind Lizzie, the flower seller with a heart of gold.

The only real thing I could do was shroud Ma and Da's grief from the massive crowds. Their sorrow was private. But I couldn't do the one thing I prayed for. I couldn't take their awful pain away. Not today. Not ever.

* * * *

The Requiem Mass over, they drifted out. Small groups of black-clad people, arms entwined, heads bowed. The bells of the church stopped as they had begun: in unison.

Never in my life had I seen such a river of people streaming toward our small house in Flinders Street. There was a smell of sadness, thick and cloying in the warm air – the scent of salty tears mixing with the heady perfume of carnations, lilies, and sweet-smelling roses, trailing all the way down Great Mersey Street. All the way back home.

I hung at the back of the crowds, strolling slowly on my own until I could no longer see anyone. A fine drizzle of rain fell, cooling the sweat on my brow. I was alone now.

I wandered lonely through our old, familiar streets. Remembering. Hearing the distant sound of Cath's laughter, her endless singing and dancing. "*Lavender's Blue, Dilly-Dilly*" played through my ears and heart. Hers had been such a sweet, innocent, melodic voice.I pictured her as a little girl, her golden ringlets, the chubby cheeks with a rosy blush.I smiled at the way she would talk to her tap shoes, bringing them to life.

I dragged myself through Lemon Street where Cath had performed a million handstands. Where she played hopscotch, and two-balls on the pawn shop wall, shouting and laughing when Punch pinched one of her prized, bouncy red balls. Beautiful memories. I turned back slowly and headed home, taking those sweet memories with me.

Ma had mentioned to me that little Clare Butt from Bootle was doing a big funeral spread for our friends and neighbours. Our house would be packed.

"She's been a godsend, has little Clare, luv. Taken care of everything, she has."

We had known the Butt family for years, although I hadn't clapped eyes on Clare since she was a little girl. They lived in Kings Park, off Stanley Road in temporary prefabs, quickly erected for those who had lost their homes in Bootle during the bombing.

It would be nice to see the Butts again after such a long time: Clare's Mum and Dad, Jinny and Johnny, and her lovely brother John who was serving as a regular in the Army.

The rain fell more heavily now, dripping off my nose when I knocked on our front door. Voices echoed from the open window and I glanced through quickly, seeing our small parlour bursting at the seams. The front door swung open as I gazed down at my wet shoes, feeling lost and alone, broken to the core.

Clare stood in front of me, smiling, though tears glistened in her lovely blue eyes. She wore a smart, elegant black dress, reaching to just below the knee. Low-heeled black shoes showed small, delicate feet. A simple pearl necklace set off her pretty young face, framed by glossy, dark-brown wavy hair.

"*Johnny!*" she cried, ushering me inside the hall and throwing her arms around me. She held me tight while I sobbed in her arms. Her grip was strong, and I felt safe.

"I'll look after you, Johnny, just you wait and see." I instantly believed her.

Clare Butt from Bootle. Kings Park prefabs.

She pushed me back, holding on to my shoulders, and looked deep into my eyes.

"Come inside, Johnny, I'll make you a nice cup of tea, luv." That sounded good, my mouth was dry as a bone.

"But, Johnny…" Clare whispered all apologetic and sorrowful, "…have yer got a shillin' for the meter, luv? Can yer believe we've bloody well run out of gas! Not a flamin' shillin' between the lot of us!"

We burst out laughing. I felt a huge weight lift off my shoulders. Clare grabbed my hand and led me through to the kitchen, and made me that nice cup of tea. We squeezed back out of the kitchen and stood huddled behind our old easy chair in the parlour.

Ma stood next the piano with Aunty Julia, where Cath had played so many times.

"Why don't you sing us a song, Ma?" I whispered softly. "She'd like that."

"Before we say goodbye to Cath?" Ma looked down at the piano.

Her smile was bittersweet and a single tear splashed down on to the keys.

"*Ain't that a shame?*" Ma quietly sang our Cath's song. My tears joined with hers, and Clare took my hand.

"Come on Johnny," she said, "let's go out for a walk."

I let her guide me through our house and in the hall she picked up a blue umbrella propped up by the coat and hat stand.

We strolled along the still, silent streets of Kirkdale. We passed the flattened ground on Stanley Road where once the Rotunda, our beautiful theatre, had stood. Hitler's bombs had laid claim to its once-grand architecture. Now, new developments had begun to crop up in the streets I loved so much. We headed up the long stretch of Kirkdale Road, stopping outside the Goat's Head on the corner. This was the pub where I played my guitar when I came home on leave, singing Country and Western songs in our group, The Dusty Road Ramblers. We were getting a bit of a following.

I sighed, watching smudgy rain pool at my feet, swirling in ever decreasing circles. Grey droplets splashed and streaked my once-shiny black shoes. Reflections of a blue sky above broke through the puddles – the tiniest glimpse of hope. Clare squeezed my hand tightly and moved closer under the umbrella. I looked up slowly and stared deeply into her face. Her eyes, full of tears above a sweet, innocent smile. A smile given with every fibre of her being – it touched my heart and soul.

I took a long, deep breath and smiled back. Falling into blue eyes crying in the rain. From somewhere else entirely a new song could be heard.

"*This could be the start of something beautiful…*"

We walked away, her strong hand holding mine. Four new steps, footprints across the sands of time.

CHAPTER 23

FIELD OF DREAMS
Carol

March 14, 1958

On that warm but windy Friday back in March 1958, my future Dad, Johnny, married kind-hearted Clare Butt from Bootle. The little lady who had the inner strength of a lion and who would later become my much-loved Mum. Her loyalty and courage were unquestionable. Her love for Johnny unconditional.

At some point in everyone's life, our inner flame is snuffed out only to be miraculously relit by a seemingly chance encounter with another human being. My future Mum was my future Dad's chance encounter. She brought with her more than her own presence when she walked into his life. He stood alone and dejected, in desperate need of love and comfort. She reignited his inner flame. Her compassionate and faithful heart restored his flagging spirit and she eased his heartache and grief. She turned his grey skies blue again and brought sunshine back into his life. Though my future Dad still loved Nora, he kept that love disguised and shared his secrets with no-one. Not then. He simply locked away his first love, hidden behind a door within his heart. He kept alive the love he had once shared with his first sweetheart Nora, in an everlasting place he would only ever visit in his dreams.

But back then he greatfully received and returned the new love my future Mum showered upon him and together they walked along a new, albeit a different path that he had once envisioned.

They embraced their marriage with high hopes for an exciting future and went on to have two children, myself and my elder

*Clare and Johnny's engagement at the Shakespeare,
with Ma, Da, Jinny and Johnny Butt.*

brother, Steve. Dad continued to play his guitar in Country and Western groups at weekends, while employed during the day as an electrician. He upheld his promise to never miss an Everton home match, and he never did. It's true what they say, laughter is infectious and grows stronger over the years. I think love is the same. Not the raucous, laugh out loud kind of way but in the steady, quiet, lifetime of dedication kind of way. I think that's how it was with my Mum and Dad and when we receive that kind of love we can never imagine life without it.

* * * *

On March 4, 2012, ten days shy of fifty-five years of marriage, bleak storms of darkness descended upon the Slater household and we were plunged into an abyss of unimaginable sorrow. Without any warning the glue that held our family together disintergrated and we stood by helpless and forlorn as our whole world fell apart. That awful, unforgettable day changed our life forever. Fifteen simple words whispered softly by the gentle ambulance man cut through my heart.

Clare and Johnny's wedding at St. Richards, 1958.

"I'm so sorry but there is nothing we can do, your Mum has gone." I wondered how it was possible to even carry on breathing when I was in so much pain.

My Dad was suddenly lost, bereft, helpless and unbelieving. "How can my little Clare Butt from Bootle be gone?" he sobbed into my arms. My eyes burned with an ache so harsh and unforgiving it ripped me apart. Together we rocked back and forth in shock and fear and pitiful disbelief. My Mum, who stood at just five feet one in her heels, was a tall woman. What she lacked in inches she made up for in character and fortitude. When she walked into a room you immediately felt her spirit, her presence was enormous. And now her absence was immeasurable. How could she be gone? She was the backbone we relied upon. She was as much a part of us as our own breath. I had no idea how we would ever pick up the pieces and be at peace again. The suddenness of her tragic death left a raw and gaping hole in many lives; Mum was loved by many. Dad lost his beautiful wife, the woman who had stood faithfully and stoically by his side through thick and thin for all these years. Never once did she ask for more than you could give. My brother and I lost a Mum we could never imagine being without. She was by best friend too, the one constant who gave so much more than she got. Her grandchildren lost the Nan they idolised, the Nan who was always there for them. The Nan who had the unique gift for making the ordinary special. Her brother and sister-in-law, my lovely Uncle John and Aunty Carol mourned the loss of their wonderful sister who they had shared so many magical adventures with. We all felt her absence in every moment. Love doesn't know its own depth until the hour of separation. My Dad was consumed with grief, we all were. It is an uphill struggle to pick yourself up and do what needs to be done, to lend your own broken shoulder to support another's heartache. But you do. You have no choice. You get up – for the sake of another. I could hear my Mum whisper, "Pick yourself up, dust yourself down and start all over again." I choked on my own broken tears.

Losing Mum brought to a head the grief and sorrow I had carried around for so long, the loss of my own beautiful son, Oliver. One of twins, he died suddenly as a young child and the pain of separation was with me every day. Now, without my Mum to prop me up, my heart – already in shreds – would never mend. Not now, not ever. I knew that for certain. But Dad had lost his other half – and so you have to somehow set aside your own grief to help someone else get through another long day. Dad was making adjustments to his life without Mum as best he could.

* * * *

*Jimmy and his future wife Claire Ainsworth at his
shipping office party after the war.*

And the rest of Dad's family? What became of them during the
fifty-five years of Dad's marriage to my Mum? Jimmy fulfilled his
dream and had a successful career as a Shipping Manager in Customs
and Excise. He read avidly throughout his life and knew everything
about anything. And he did eventually get a proper drum kit, and
finally threw away the old saucepans he practised on as a teenager. He
married, and had three lovely children.

Ma and Aunty Julia carried on telling jokes and hilarious stories,
singing and playing the piano into their eighties. Da finally retired
from the Merchant Navy but sadly died not long after. Dad also lost
his faithful friend, Punch, who simply went out one day and never
came back. He cried buckets for the four-legged friend who had been
so much a part of his life during the War Years. Deep down, he still
believes Punch never really died, but simply walked off into another
world where he's still playing with a new gang of kids, giving them
the same adventures he gave Dad and his childhood mates. Giving a
whole new gang of deserving kids the unconditional love which a dog
gives so freely.

Our friend Fran outside our house in
Flinders Street after the war.

Ma and Aunty Julia stayed in Flinders Street until the late Sixties, when demolition of some of the terraced streets in the shadows of Kirkdale took place. Today there lies a green, open space where once stood the Slaters' old home. A living, green field replaces the homes of his family, friends and neighbours. A place where memories live on for my Dad. His 'Field of Dreams', he calls it. A place where he can stand quietly and reflect; relive memories and past, distant dreams.

It is the place he will always call home.

EPILOGUE
Carol

19 May, 2012

It had only been two months since we said goodbye to Mum. It was my birthday and Mum always made such a big fuss of birthdays, insisting we always celebrated no matter what was going on in our lives. For Dad, it would be the first of his children's birthdays without my mum at his side. I would celebrate with him and make a big fuss, although it was the last thing I wanted to do.

Armed with a bag of strawberries, a bottle of Buck's Fizz, fresh cream, flowers, pastries and a brand-new tablecloth, I headed up to Dad's for a birthday breakfast celebration.

He opened the door, smiling, his eyes sparkling, dressed-up and looking fresh as a daisy. In fact, he looked the best I had seen him for two months. I set the table and laid out our birthday banquet. Dad was lively, excited, and couldn't keep still. I could see he was itching to tell me something.

He began to tell me his story. I could never have imagined in a million years what he was about to reveal over that birthday breakfast.

Dad likes a flutter on the horses. Fifty-pence bets in his Coral betting shop in Ormskirk, where he now lives with us. He meets up with his mates and they ponder which horse will come in first. But Dad doesn't bet on form, he doesn't track the horse's performance. He uses his old, tried and tested method of 'meaningful coincidence'; synchronicity. He studies the horses' names, jockeys, colours and numbers, all of which he believes hold hidden signs and messages that can show us the right path towards our destiny.

On this day, 18 May 2012 – one day before my birthday – as he leafed through the names of the horses, Dad noticed such a sign.

We've all experienced those uncanny coincidences at one time or another. An unlikely sequence of events that occurs simultaneously, or what seems like a destined chain of events that happens without warning, or at 'just the right time'. This type of synchronicity can seem startling and mysterious. You think of someone for the first time in years and run into them a few hours later. An unusual phrase you'd never heard before jumps out at you three times in the same day. In the back street of a foreign land while on holiday you bump into an old friend from school. '*There are no accidents*', as the popular saying has it; everything you experience is perfectly orchestrated.

As he scanned the horses' names that day in the betting shop, Dad realised with a start that two of them were called 'Broughton Silk' and 'Broughton Hat'. His lost love, Nora, went to Broughton Hall College in Liverpool. The navy blue and gold silk ribbons on the jockey were the same colours as the college hat Nora wore, about which he teased her when he met her off the tram each night.

He placed his bet, thinking of Nora and the love he had never lost for her. The horse won, coming in at six to one.

Dad carried on with his story…

On his way home from the betting shop he bought a *Liverpool Echo*, as he does every day. At home, he couldn't stop thinking about Nora while he turned the pages. He realised suddenly, at that point, that he would never, ever – in this life or the next – forget the beautiful woman he knew and had loved since he was thirteen years old. The feelings that came back were feelings that had never truly left.

As he turned to the Obituaries in the *Echo*, Nora's surname leapt out at him. Reading on, he realised her sister had died. Nora and her daughter had included a tribute, but there was no mention of a husband's name for Nora. He hadn't seen her in fifty-eight years and wondered if she was widowed. He decided there and then to find her. And he did, that very same night. After many phone calls and searching he discovered Nora had returned to Snowdrop Street when her husband died and now lived with her daughter. He miraculously found Nora's phone number after all these years. Dad made the call –and his whole life changed in an instant. They talked for hours, long into the night. They opened up their hearts to each other and shed many tears of loss and regret. Nora had never lost the love she had for my Dad and just like him she too had kept it hidden behind a locked door within her heart for 58 years. They arranged to meet the very next day to pick up where they had left such a long time ago.

There's something romantically bittersweet about an old flame. As if by magic you are reconnected quickly, together again, as if you had never parted. Dad said he fell in love with her when they were together, then fell deeper in love with her in the years apart.

"True love," he said. "Doesn't mean you will never part. It just means you will always get back together. It might take a year, it might take fifty-eight, but what's meant to be will always find its way. Nothing and no-one can end true love. We may get lost for a while on our journey, but real love will always conquer, and eventually reunite. That's the beauty of true love, you always end up with the right person at the right time, regardless of any other factor."

All those years ago, when Dad and Nora were meant to meet in their usual place to decide the fate of their love, it seems their stars were well and truly crossed. Nora was held up at work and sent a young lad from her office to meet Dad and pass on a note, saying she would be on the next tram. The young lad never did deliver that note. Dad had left by the time Nora eventually arrived, and of course she thought it meant he wanted to end their relationship. She, too, had loved Johnny Slater for all of these years.

It must be said that Dad's revelations weren't without their challenges for family and friends. How could they not be, when we were so fresh in grief for our lovely mum, nan, sister and friend? But I wished Dad and Nora happiness as they followed their hearts, and as they planned their wedding, the light in Dads eye's sparkled once more. Together they walked new roads, made new paths with their older footprints across the sands of time. Hand in hand they sat and dreamed across the red gingham tablecloth in Pierre's restaurant in Liverpool. The candlelight flickered, dancing across their smiling faces. The lost years melted away in loves new embrace. They revisted old, familiar places and laughed at the memories so easily recalled. And they danced freely, unabashed in their own special place just like they did all those long lonely years ago. They strolled along the famous Matthew Street, home to the Cavern were the Beatles once played. When the Cavern was rebuilt in the 1970s a section of its original brick was inscribed with every group that had ever played there. Dad pointed out to Nora "The Dusty Road Ramblers" the group he played guitar with, sharing a stage with the Beatles all those years ago. "We'll have years together now Johnny and you can play your guitar to me whenever you want." Nora laughed. "We have a lot of time to catch up with." They vowed to treasure each and every new moment with their second chance of happiness. For seven glorious months they hadn't stopped smiling or counting their blessings at finding each other again.

Dad walked happily and excitedly along Stanley Road towards Snowdrop Street. He was taking Nora to a new restaurant in town today to talk more about their wedding plans. As he rounded the corner he stopped in his tracks at the sight of an ambulance outside Nora's house. He dropped his bag holding Nora's favourite cake. As the ambulance drove away, Nora's daughter and the neighbours came rushing to my Dad's side. He sobbed uncontrollably at the devasting news. His sweetheart from Snowdrop Street had suddenly passed away, waiting in her chair by the window, all dressed up to go out for lunch with my Dad. "A massive heart attack," the neighbours said. Dad had missed Nora's last goodbye by minutes. He was broken, desolate and torn apart. He felt his heart being ripped out. No words, no actions, would ever bring comfort to a broken soul. How could it?

Once again he mourned the loss of true love's brief encounter. But over time he realised he was grateful too, for those seven brief months which – for him – could have been seven years or seventy, for he believes it is not yet over for him and Nora. From his heart, he says, "someday, somewhere, we will meet again, and share our eternal, everlasting love."

Their story, in the circle of life, is not yet complete.

APPENDIX

LETTERS FROM AUNT JULIA

Flinders Street
Kirkdale
Liverpool

February 1941

Dear Johnny,
Your Punch is having a ball, son. I tell you what Johnny, between Punch and Judy I haven't got much room left in my bed. I can hardly turn over

And I tell you something else, my God, Punch can't half snore. I swear to God he makes the windows rattle.

Punch and Judy are the best Dog Patrollers ever. They check up on the neighbours twice a day. I think they enjoy their wages, really. Treats from every house. Twice a day! They look like a pair of stuffed cushions.

Oh… I was out in the street brushing my front when that scruffy mongrel from Commercial Road strutted past. Didn't he just go and bloody well pinch Punch's hat? Whipped it straight off his head, the hard-faced so-and-so.

Well, I wasn't having that!

I chased after that scruffy mongrel with me yard brush. Right down our street! Can yer believe he was trying to bury Punch's hat in a pile of old rubble? I tell yer what, luv, if he was my dog I'd shave his arse and teach him to walk backwards. He soon scarpered and dropped the hat when I showed him the bottom of me yard brush. I was a bit out of breath by the time I got home.

His hat was a bit mucky but I soon scrubbed it up and Punch is happy again. I made the chin strap a bit tighter. No danger of his hat being pinched again. .

I do think it's shrunk a bit. Either that or his head's grown. I bet your Ma says I've been feeding him too many biscuits. Awww, but he does love a biscuit and who can say no to a face like that? Act soft and I'll buy you a coal yard. That's your Punch! His face would get him the parish. Awww, but I love him to bits and he is doing great, luv.

Well that's it for now, Johnny,

Ta-ra luv,

Aunty Julia, Punch and Judy

* * * *

September 1941

Dear Johnny,

I bumped into that teacher of yours the other day, luv. The one you call Rusty behind her back? She must've got that nickname on account of all that flaming red hair of hers I suppose? Doesn't she look like Rita Hayworth from the movies? I do know you've got a soft spot for her! I bet yer didn't know I knew that. Well I do! And there's nothing wrong with a crush, luv. Mind you, I think she's got her eye on you on the quiet. I bet yer teacher's pet. Oh you'll have me guts for garters now won't yer, lad? Anyway, she was outside Daisy Street School. We were having a lovely little natter till that other teacher butted in. That snooty, bossy one. Marmie Marks! She's what you'd call a proper tuppence ha'penny toff, luv. Is it me, Johnny? Or does her face really hang like a wet nellie? That voice of hers doesn't half get me back up. You'd think she had a gob full of marbles. But God help her lad, I imagine the only place she's ever invited to is outside.

Anyway, the teachers were about to have a committee meeting. And didn't I go and get meself invited in! Oooh, the state of me and the price of fish! I felt like a queen.

Sister Gonzaga was in charge, luv. She's a lovely nun, one of the best. I had to strain me ears to catch what she was saying though. She speaks all gentle and quiet like. Either that or I'm going as deaf as a post. Yer know, I swear Sister Gonzaga was wearing a golden halo.

Well anyway, it seems the committee was deciding what to do with the kids from St. Alphonsus' School. As yer know it was flattened by Hitler's bombs.

They're going to put all the school-less kids in with you lot at Daisy Street. Yer'll have to squeeze up and make a bit of room in your classrooms. Mind you, I don't know how it's all going to work out, what with them being Protestant and you lot Catholic. Oh, but that doesn't really matter, does it, luv. Were all in the same boat at the end of the day.

School will be a bit different when yer get back. Yer'll make loads of new friends, Johnny. It'll be great for everyone, mark my words.

Can yer believe that your Punch and Judy are still snoring an farting in me bed? At this time of day! No more pea soup for them! Smells like a pea factory in here.

Awww, but they were out late again last night on Dog Patrol. Doing a fantastic job, they are. I'll let them have a nice sleep in. Mrs Turner from number twenty-two gave them two ham shank bones. They were a bit miffed when I wouldn't let them suck the bones in me bed. Oh, speak of the devil. Here's the pair of them now trotting down the dancers. I expect they want breakfast. Better dash before they start howling.

Ta-ra luv,

Aunty Julia, Punch and Judy

ACKNOWLEDGMENTS

AND PERMISSIONS

This is a work of creative non-fiction. The events are portrayed to the best of Johnny Slater's memory. While all the stories in this book are true, some names, and identifying details – apart from immediate family – have been changed to protect the privacy of the people involved. Everything here is true, but it may not be entirely factual. In some cases we have compressed events; in others we have made two people into one. We have occasionally embroidered. We have learnt over time that the most important thing in life is telling a good tale.

Memories of historical events recalled by 85-year-old Johnny can sometimes blur. For the purpose of historical education and for those who did not live through the war years, facts have been sourced and included in some of the narrative.

It takes a lot of research when compiling someone's memory of events. We would like to thank all the kind people who have graciously helped and pointed us in the right direction. With due diligence we have endeavoured to seek permission for the use of photographs, images, and the many sources of reference.

We thank the internet for its endless supply of information … what did we do in the days before Google and Wikipedia?

Thank you also to the following:

The Picton Library, Liverpool Historic Society, Liverpool
   Blitz, B.B.C History
Eyewitness to History, John Carey
*Britain, Egypt and the Middle East: imperial policy in the
   aftermath of the war 1918-1922*, John Darwin

Britain and Decolonization, John Darwin

If we have failed to acknowledge anyone, it is due to human error and not intention, please let us know and we will rectify immediately. It has been quite a challenge marrying fact with memories, we have done our best to name all the help received and we thank you all from the bottom of our hearts.

Carol Wainwright
madmotherturtle@yahoo.co.uk
www.memoriesofliverpool.co.uk
Face Book: Carol Wainwright

Suggested FB groups for more memories:
I'm from Kirkdale
and
Liverpool Happy Memories.